GREAT PASSENGER SHIPS
1910-1920

GREAT PASSENGER SHIPS 1910-1920

WILLIAM H. MILLER

The
History
Press

For David Perry & Alfredo Casuso

*Dearest of friends, great ship enthusiasts,
ocean cruisers and creative wizards*

First published 2011

The History Press
The Mill, Brimscombe Port
Stroud, Gloucestershire, GL5 2QG
www.thehistorypress.co.uk

© William H. Miller, 2011

British Library Cataloguing in Publication Data.
A catalogue record for this book is available from the British Library.

ISBN 978 0 7524 5663 8

Typesetting and origination by The History Press
Printed in Great Britain
Manufacturing managed by Jellyfish Print Solutions Ltd

CONTENTS

ACKNOWLEDGEMENTS

Any book is very much a joint effort. As I have so often noted and written, I am more of the 'cruise director' of a book project. Like the entertainments and diversions onboard ships, I gather a series of assistants, generous and kind souls who offer information, reflections, anecdotes and, in a class by themselves, the photographs and illustrations. The photos are, in ways, the steel frame around which the book itself is assembled and then brought to completion.

First, I must thank Emily Locke and Amy Rigg at The History Press for their splendid assistance, cooperation and support. Both are much like 'first officers' in a book project such as this. They take the initial version from me and then develop, refine and polish it all. In the end, they bring it to a finished product. I must also thank two very good, longtime friends. Bill Muller, one of the finest maritime artists of this time, has generously loaned material for the front as well as rear cover. Indeed, they are brilliant, eye-catching additions to the finished book. Then, Charles Haas has provided a well-written, insightful Foreword. I am much in debt to both gentlemen.

Equally valuable and wonderfully generous, two other longtime friends, Richard Faber and Albert Wilhelmi, have so generously and patiently loaned a great selection of very interesting, largely unpublished and therefore unseen photos. A huge nod of thanks to both of them.

Pine Hodges and Stanley Lehrer both provided more than the usual anecdote and comment, but also considerable additions to the understanding of the great liners of 1910–20.

Further, grateful assistance came from Ernest Arroyo, the late Frank O. Braynard, Philippe Brebant, Luis Miguel Correia, the late Alex Duncan, James Giammatteo, Laire Jose Giraud, Michael Hadgis, Des Kirkpatrick, Arnold Kludas, Norman Knebel, Anthony La Forgia, the late Abe Michaelson, Richard K. Morse, John Nesbitt, Hayao Nogami, Hisashi Noma, the late James Sesta, the late Victor Scrivens and V.H. Young. Organisations that have assisted include the Cunard Line, French Liner, Hapag-Lloyd, Shaw Savill Line and the United States Lines.

If, for some oversight, I have failed to mention someone, my sincere apologies in advance.

FOREWORD

The decade from 1910–1920 saw great change in many facets of daily life. Technology, in the ascendant, promised better futures. Social issues, medicine, literature, education – progress touched them all.

On the world's oceans, a veritable flood of human beings was revolutionising travel. Some 14 million immigrated to the United States during the decade, seeking refuge, opportunity, or perhaps 'streets paved with gold'.

To carry these 'huddled masses', as well as the titans of business, professionals and a rising middle class, the world's steamship companies – particularly those engaged in the lucrative North Atlantic trade – engaged in a building programme without parallel. Progress in propulsion machinery provided the ever-higher speeds the travelling public demanded. Accommodations for the humblest immigrant, evolving from the dank terrors of dormitory-like areas in steerage to separate cabins with stewards at one's call, reflected shipowners' realisation that immigrants generated the greatest per-head profit. Second-class accommodations rivalled the first class of just a decade earlier. First class reached new heights of luxury and exceptional service.

The result was a veritable parade of great liners that today, a century later, still awe us with their beauty and technical innovation. Built in the shipyards of Great Britain, France and Germany, the vessels were both evolutionary and revolutionary. The *Olympic*, *Titanic* and *Britannic*; *Lusitania*, *Mauretania* and *Aquitania*; the *France*; and the *Vaterland*, *Imperator* and *Bismarck* – their names among the greatest and most loved liners, the apotheosis of twentieth-century builders' and decorators' craft, floating ambassadors of national pride.

Tragedy beset this decade, which had begun so optimistically. *Titanic* – perhaps the most famous liner of all – did not complete her maiden voyage, sunk by an iceberg off the Grand Banks with shocking loss of life, a victim of complacency and overconfidence.

Consuming nearly half of the decade, the First World War transformed luxurious liners into sombre hospital ships, armed merchant cruisers, troop transports – and victims of torpedoes and mines. After the conflict, many surviving vessels reappeared under new flags and with new names.

Over four decades, in more than eighty books, and in his lectures ashore and aboard the world's cruise ships, Bill Miller, maritime history's most eminent contributor, has enthralled and educated tens of thousands with his superb research, his consummate knowledge and his scintillating style at the podium.

In bringing his expertise to telling the story of the liners of this fascinating decade, Bill takes us on yet another fascinating journey, to a time of triumph and tragedy, optimism and loss, progress and setback. In doing so, he reminds us of the qualities that make some ships truly 'great', and the historian's vital role in ensuring that long after they've sailed their last mile, their places in history are remembered.

Charles A. Haas
President, Titanic International Society
Co-author, *Titanic: Triumph and Tragedy*

INTRODUCTION

This book comes, to a great extent, at just the right time. We are on the eve of the centennial of the most famous sea disaster of all time, involving the most famous ship of all time. It is, of course, the *Titanic*. This infamous liner was created at the very beginning of the decade of our title and then lost on 14–15 April 1912. Yes, through books, continuing research, films, TV documentaries and even a Broadway musical, the subject of the 'unsinkable' ship that actually sinks, and on her maiden voyage no less, is alive and well. The centennial will bring, I am quite sure, a new surge of interest – through exhibitions, further books, commemorative cruises and the hint (at the time of writing) that *Titanic*, the 1997 mega-spectacular film, might be reissued, but bigger and even better. Will we see *Titanic* in 3D? The public fascination with the doomed ship and the horrific tragedy seems never to end. As for me, as presents for Christmas 2010, I received three new books about the White Star liner.

The decade 1910–1920 was truly dramatic. It was the Industrial Age reaching for new heights, new dimensions, breaking records. Ocean liners, as an example, were becoming bigger and longer and taller and faster. On board the larger liners, they were also certainly becoming grander – indeed, it was the age of the 'floating palace'. It was also an age of increased corporate rivalries as well as political ones. It seemed to be a continuous swing between Imperial Britain and Imperial Germany in the game of 'Who could build the bigger ship?' The ever-industrious and inventive Germans truly tipped the scales in 1913 with the extraordinary *Imperator*. How astonishing she was then at over 52,000 tons, over 900ft in length and carrying nearly 5,000 passengers! But everyone, it seemed, was building bigger and bigger ships – even away from the famed North Atlantic run, prominent shipping companies such as P&O to Australia, Union-Castle to Africa and Royal Mail to South America were constructing enormous vessels.

It all changed, however, following the high drama at Sarajevo in the summer of 1914. The First World War erupted. Commercial trading was all but suspended completely and instead ships took on new roles: ferrying troops and munitions; serving in different and varied roles such as armed merchant cruisers, hospital ships, and at least one was even converted to an aircraft carrier. Through to the Armistice of November 1918, they were horribly destructive times as well. The sinking of the *Lusitania* is perhaps the best remembered. And they were also disruptive years: Germany's super ships – the *Imperator*, *Vaterland* and *Bismarck* – found themselves flying British and American flags by the war's end. Mighty firms such as Hamburg America and North German Lloyd lost just about everything while Cunard, White Star and others had to rebuild, revive, almost reinvent themselves for a return to peacetime operations in 1919–20.

Yes, without question it was a very interesting decade. The great growth of ships would seem to be the main theme. Ocean liners were bigger and better than ever. And in many ways, the future hinted of even greater sizes. Now, nearly a century later, we have come to the age of the likes of 225,000grt, 6,400-passenger mega-sisters *Oasis of the Seas* and *Allure of the Seas*. The luxurious amenities of elevators, indoor pools and the first barber's shop chair of a century ago have given way to today's shipboard ice-skating rinks, rock climbing walls and cross-deck ziplines. Clearly, those 'floating palaces' of 1910–20 were just the beginning.

Bill Miller
Secaucus, New Jersey
2011

1

FLOATING PALACES OF THE ATLANTIC

Between continents! On a summer's afternoon in 2010, I visited (and for the second time in two years) the famed Harland & Wolff shipyard at Belfast in Northern Ireland. Although two huge gantry cranes hovered about, it was a much reduced facility. The slipways had long been empty and work sheds seemed quiet, while all-but-derelict structures from a century ago were earmarked for new, revitalised hotel, conference and recreational purposes. And, of course, connected directly to the immortal *Titanic*, there is also tourism. The yard had long since ceased building ships (their last liner, P&O's *Canberra*, was completed there in 1961) and turned then to ship repair as well as specialty works (such as creating large wind fans). All rather silent, several large but otherwise nondescript sheds handled, it seemed, the current needs of the once-booming plant. Belfast was once, of course, one of the capitals of ocean liner creation and construction. Three of the world's largest liners, the *Olympic*, *Titanic* and *Britannic*, were built there between 1911–15.

The North Atlantic run to America was the busiest, most profitable and assuredly most competitive passenger ship route in the world. Hundreds of ships plied those northern seas, sailing not only from the likes of Liverpool, Southampton, Bremerhaven and Hamburg, but also Copenhagen, Gdynia, Rotterdam and Antwerp. They crossed mostly to New York, but also to other ports such as Montreal, Quebec City, Halifax, Boston and Philadelphia. There was even a regular passenger service to Portland, Maine.

The biggest, fastest and grandest liners plied the North Atlantic. It was, by 1910, very much the age of the 'floating palaces', large and luxurious ships that vied with one another for their share of lucrative passenger traffic as well as prestige and publicity. Almost everyone, it seemed, wanted to travel on the biggest and fastest liners, and of course the newest as well. First-class accommodations grew increasingly grander, even more opulent, and even more amenity-filled. Second class, a sort of ocean-going 'business class', became more comfortable. But it was third class that garnered the greatest (if quietest) interest. With over a million passengers going westbound to the New World each year, it was the most lucrative.

By 1910, the world's largest liners were a growing collection. The first of the celebrated four-stackers were still about: the *Kaiser Wilhelm der Grosse*, *Deutschland*, *Kronprinz Wilhelm*, *Kaiser Wilhelm II* and *Kronprinzessin Cecilie*. These proud Germans were countered, to some extent, by British liners: White Star's 'Big Four' – *Celtic*, *Cedric*, *Baltic* and *Adriatic*. A great turning point came in 1907 when Cunard seemed to pull out all stops with the 31,000grt near-sisters *Lusitania* and *Mauretania*. They were quickly dubbed 'the greatest ships in the world' and were hugely successful from the start. The ships were Britain's first four-stackers, a design element that tended to greatly impress the travelling public as symbols of size, power and strength. If three-stackers were much preferred, four-stackers were thought of as the 'safest' way to cross the great Atlantic. On the inside, in first class, accommodations on these great Cunarders were likened to an English country house. They were indeed palatial: the fittings and fixtures included an Edwardian restaurant, gilding and polished-wood panelling, a glass skylight and even a tree-filled verandah café. There were also crystal chandeliers, thick carpets and deeply cushioned sofas. Some even began referring to the two liners as being like 'grand hotels that moved'.

The *Lusitania* and *Mauretania* were, of course, only the beginning. They seemed to ignite an even greater race in ocean liner design, style, size and of course speed. Political rivalries, particularly between Britain and Germany, seemed also to heighten. Owning the biggest and fastest liner seemed to be a prime element in national prestige; that gilded imagery and those early public relations of national prominence.

Above Preparation for sailing: the great *Lusitania*, the first of the four-funnel Cunarders and the first under the British flag, is seen here at the Princes Landing Stage, Liverpool. (Albert Wilhelmi Collection)

The Greyhound of the Ocean :—
Record Passage (long route), 4 days, 20 hours, 22 minutes.
Highest Day's Run, 632.   Average Speed 24·83 knots.

The Cunard Liner
LUSITANIA

Right Maritime might: this view of the *Lusitania* is entitled 'The Greyhound of the Ocean' and notes the ship's record run of four days, twenty hours and twenty-two minutes between England and the United States. (Albert Wilhelmi Collection)

Crowds gather along the Princes Landing Stage to see off the towering *Lusitania*. (Albert Wilhelmi Collection)

Ocean power: the splendid *Lusitania* seen at high speed with all four funnels in use. (Richard Faber Collection)

The *Mauretania* remains one of the greatest, most popular and most successful liners of the twentieth century. According to ocean liner historian and keen passenger ship observer Pine Hodges:

The *Maury*, as she was so lovingly dubbed, had a number of 'firsts'; among them was the first barber shop chair on a liner and the first installation of decorative elevator grille-work made from aluminium alloy. The ship and her sister, the *Lusitania*, often referred as the *Lucy*, were also the very first liners to have en suite cabins with private bathroom facilities. The *Mauretania* also had several so-called 'fanlight' windows in her second-class lounge. These windows, plus the private bathrooms, created a benchmark and were greatly expanded upon, four years later, in the new *Olympic*-class liners, which were fitted with large numbers of these windows and many more private baths in first class. The Veranda Café on both the *Mauretania* and *Lusitania* quickly evolved as well, into the larger, dual Palm Courts onboard the *Olympic*. Although the *Olympic*'s dining rooms were single height, as opposed to those on the *Mauretania,* grandeur was more than made up for in the *Olympic*'s sweeping Grand Staircase. Also, even second class had their own elevator.

Transatlantic passenger loads, even in the depths of cold, storm-tossed winters, seemed to increase. Prompted by those two big Cunarders, rival White Star Line turned, by 1908–09, to building three giant liners for their express run between Southampton and New York. Cunard, it seemed, would wait for a time before planning their largest liner yet, a third ship for weekly sailings in each direction, that would become the *Aquitania*, completed in 1914. The Germans paused slightly with the likes of the 25,600grt *George Washington*. But in Hamburg, plans were well underway for the biggest liners yet built, the first of which, the very first ship to exceed a then mind-boggling 50,000 tons, would come into service in 1913. Two

even larger ships would follow at yearly intervals. The Germans, it appeared, would have the top ships for some years to come.

Business boomed, of course. On some days, over a dozen passenger ships arrived in New York from European ports. New ships were coming out of shipyards at a brisk pace. Many of them were more moderate, intermediate passenger ships and not the well-documented, best-remembered superliners. Befitting one of the biggest passenger ship firms, Cunard was almost always adding new tonnage. Capped by twin funnels, the 18,000-ton sisters *Franconia* and *Laconia* were added in 1910–11, but primarily for the supplemental Liverpool–Boston service. These ships were soon followed by a trio, the 2,200-passenger *Andania*, *Alaunia* and *Aurania*, created especially for the seasonal Liverpool–Montreal service (the ships were detoured, however, to Halifax and Boston in winter). The Allan Line tipped the scales by building the biggest passenger ships yet for the Canadian run, the 18,500-ton, 600ft-long sisters *Alsatian* and *Calgarian*. That ever-expanding transportation network, Canadian Pacific Steamships, reinforced its Montreal service with new ships such as the 1,800-passenger sister ships *Missanabie* and *Metagama*.

There were other smaller transatlantic ships such as Trieste-based Union Austriaca's 12,500grt *Kaiser Franz Josef I*. Her role was mostly to look after the lucrative immigrant trade to America. Anchor Line added two new ships, the *Transylvania* and *Tuscania*, commissioned in 1914, and intended for a joint Mediterranean–New York service with the Cunard Line. The French-flag Fabre Line added two three-stackers, the sisters *Patria* and *Providence*, with over 2,100 berths in three classes each. They too were used in Mediterranean–New York service. Norwegian America Line arrived on the transatlantic scene with its very first ships, both to be used on the Oslo–Copenhagen–New York route. The 10,700-ton *Kristianafjord* arrived first, in May 1913, and then months later was followed by the *Bergensfjord*. The latter enjoyed a very long and diverse career, sailing for forty-six years in all.

Ready for launching, this view of the *Mauretania*, dated September 1906, shows the 790ft-long ship ready for launching at the Swan, Hunter & Wigham Richardson shipyard at Newcastle. Her beautiful counter stern is most evident in this scene. (Albert Wilhelmi Collection)

Fitting out: the 31,938grt *Mauretania* is being fitted out at Newcastle and readied for her maiden crossing to New York in November 1907. (Albert Wilhelmi Collection)

Above With a capacity of 2,335 passengers divided into three classes and with a crew of 812, the ever-beautiful *Mauretania* is seen arriving in the Hudson River at New York. (Cronican-Arroyo Collection)

Left The expansive second-class sports deck as seen at the *Mauretania*'s Pier 56 berth at New York. Another Cunarder, the *Scythia*, is seen to the right. (Cronican-Arroyo Collection)

Afternoon sailing: the *Mauretania* outbound at New York in a view dated 1931. (Richard Faber Collection)

Classic style: White Star's 'Big Four' – which included the *Baltic*, seen here outbound at Liverpool – used the exterior form of four tall masts. (Richard Faber Collection)

Between voyages: the *Samaria* (left) and *Mauretania* (right) at Cunard's New York terminal in the 1920s. (Victor Scrivens Collection)

The *Adriatic* being 'worked' by cargo barges at New York in a photo dating from 1925. (Port Authority of New York & New Jersey)

Above The 18,150grt *Franconia* was built for Cunard's Liverpool–Boston service. Completed in 1911, she was torpedoed and sunk in October 1916 when only five years old. (Richard Faber Collection)

Right Cunard's 'A Class', including the *Andania, Alaunia* (seen here at Boston) and the *Aurania*, was created in 1913. Sadly, each of these 13,400grt ships was a casualty of the First World War. (Richard Faber Collection)

Above The 540ft-long *Andania* and her sisters were designed to sail to Montreal in the summers and to Boston in the winter. The ship is seen here, in a view dated 21 August 1913, departing from Southampton. (Albert Wilhelmi Collection)

Left Canada bound: the 14,900grt *Megantic*, commissioned in 1909 for White Star Line's Liverpool–Montreal service, was originally intended to be the *Albany* for the Dominion Line. (Richard Faber Collection)

Left Cunard's *Saxonia* and her sister *Ivernia*, completed in 1900, had two of the largest funnels ever to put to sea. The 600ft-long *Saxonia* is seen here loading passengers at the Landing Stage, Liverpool. (Richard Faber Collection)

Below Mishap: the 526ft-long *Slavonia*, built in 1902 especially for Cunard's Mediterranean–New York trade, had a shortened career. On a crossing to Trieste, she was grounded in the Azores, in June 1910, and became a complete loss. (Richard Faber Collection)

Above Varied career: after the Second World War, the *Bergensfjord* was sold to the Home Lines and became their *Argentina*. In 1953, she became the first large liner in the infant Israeli merchant marine, sailing for the Zim Lines as the *Jerusalem*. She was later renamed *Aliya* before being scrapped in 1959, completing a career of forty-six years. The 530ft-long ship is seen here with the Lower Manhattan skyline in the background. (Author's Collection)

Left The 11,000-ton *Bergensfjord* was the second passenger ship for the newly created Norwegian America Line and their Atlantic service between Oslo, Copenhagen, Bergen, Stavanger and New York. The ship is seen, in a photo dated 16 November 1938, in New York's Lower Bay, having departed from her berth at the lower end of the Brooklyn waterfront. (Cronican-Arroyo Collection)

Right The 10,000grt *Hellig Olav* was built in 1903 for Denmark's Det Forenede, known also as the Scandinavian-American Line, for their Copenhagen–New York service. (Author's Collection)

Below Allan Line's *Virginian*, completed in 1905, became the *Drottningholm* of the Swedish America Line in 1920. She is shown here outbound from New York, wearing neutrality markings, in the autumn of 1939. (Richard Faber Collection)

Above The 17,600grt *Lapland*, built in 1909, was used in Red Star Line's Antwerp-New York service. Seen here arriving at New York, the *President Roosevelt* of the United States Lines is outbound on the right. (Gillespie-Faber Collection)

Left The French-flag *Providence*, owned by the Fabre Line, was completed on the very eve of the start in the First World War, in the spring of 1914. The 11,900-tonner was used in the Marseilles–New York service. (Richard Faber Collection)

Left Diverse career: the 13,600grt *Mongolia* was built in 1903 for the North Atlantic services of the Atlantic Transport Line, but instead was diverted to transpacific duties. She later returned to the Atlantic, running London–New York crossings. She became the *President Fillmore* of the Dollar Line in 1926 and is seen in this view along the Brooklyn waterfront. (Author's Collection)

Below Another mishap: Canadian Pacific's 12,400grt *Metagama*, used on the Glasgow–Montreal run, ran aground in the St Lawrence River. Later repaired, she sailed until broken up in 1934. (Author's Collection)

2

WHITE STAR'S TRIO

The White Star Line was in its greatest period in the first decade of the twentieth century. Although under the control of J. Pierpont Morgan's International Mercantile Marine – the IMM, for short – it became the senior firm of that large consortium. In a special arrangement, their ships were allowed to fly the British flag despite their American ownership. The White Star corporate policy was to continue at the forefront of Atlantic passenger shipping, but minus one principal element: they were not interested in great speed or breaking any existing speed records. Instead, their emphasis was threefold: great size, luxurious if not very comfortable accommodations and moderate speed. White Star was, of course, deeply challenged by the first appearance of the speedy *Lusitania* and *Mauretania* in 1907. Cunard was, quite apparently, their greatest rival. Consequently, White Star looked to build three giant liners, but not for the six-night Liverpool–New York express run, but instead the six-day runs based at Southampton. The new trio, in cooperation with a long-time company friend, Harland & Wolff Ltd, the Belfast-based shipbuilders, would be 45,000-tonners compared to the 31,000 tons of *Lusitania* and *Mauretania*. It was, after all, all about size. The public simply loved the biggest liners and nothing was better than the very largest.

The very early plan was to name the three liners as *Gigantic*, *Titanic* and *Olympic*. But names were soon swapped – the *Olympic* was to be the first ship. She was ceremoniously launched on 20 October 1910. Invited dignitaries and other guests were more than excited, even intrigued. At the launching, they could gaze across the building slipway and see the early steel frames of the second of the sisters, the *Titanic*.

Befitting the largest liner in the world, both the London and New York offices of White Star worked especially hard to create enthusiasm, both in the shipping community and amongst the travelling public. Great, detailed attention was paid to the outstanding, even innovative level of luxury and comfort that would be found aboard the new liner. Descriptions included the Arabian indoor swimming pool (the very first on a transatlantic liner) complete with bronze lamps and even an ornate marble drinking fountain. The first-class staterooms were decorated in no fewer than eleven different styles of décor and the lush greenery in the Palm Court was more like a landside club, a lush retreat. Reflective of the times and White Star's marketing plans, there were an unusually high 1,054 beds in first class. Businessmen commuting between the continents and wealthy tourists on grand tours were among those travellers sought for the *Olympic* and her sisters. More moderately, there were also 510 berths in second class.

Westbound immigration was a boom business and so there were 1,020 berths down in third class aboard the *Olympic*. These were often booked to capacity. Of the liner's four towering funnels, only three actually dispensed smoke. The fourth was a dummy, used as a ventilator, but also adding to the vessel's image of grandeur, reliability and safety. Immigrants very often judged a ship's safety by the number of the funnels. A four-funnel ship was said to be the safest way for the 'voyage of a lifetime'.

White Star's greatest and possibly proudest day was 31 May 1911. A great number of guests arrived at Belfast for the noontime launching of the *Titanic*. Then, in the afternoon, they boarded the gleaming, brand new *Olympic*, which soon departed for an overnight voyage down to Southampton. The company could not have created a better effect or stronger image. The 45,324grt *Olympic* left Southampton on 14 June, proudly dressed overall in flags and listed as the largest ship of any kind. The record passed to the 46,329grt *Titanic* a year later and then, in 1913, to the 52,117grt *Imperator*. By the eve of the First World War, in the summer of 1914, the honour was held by the 54,282grt *Vaterland*.

The splendid *Olympic*, the first of White Star's three 'floating palaces'. (Richard Faber Collection)

According to Pine Hodges:

The *Olympic* & *Titanic* were structurally and mechanically identical, and very nearly so decoratively. In addition to the glassed-in forward A Deck Promenade, the bridge-wings extended a few feet further on the *Titanic*. While the *Olympic* had a second, full-length Promenade along B Deck, the same space on the *Titanic* became larger cabins, extended out to the ship's side. Two 50ft sections of the Promenade were retained as Private Promenades for two Parlor Suites. Aft on B Deck was the A la Carte Restaurant, which was extended into the port Promenade during the *Olympic's* first major refit in 1913, and as was done earlier on the *Titanic*. The Café Parisien was added at the same time in the starboard B Deck Promenade as the *Titanic* had, but was more 'finished'. The dining rooms on both ships were identical except that the *Titanic's* had carpeting. Even small

details differed. The *Olympic's* Grand Staircase had an extra, light metal handrail added atop the massive oak balustrades, allowing passengers an easier grasp in rough weather.

Titanica! Interest was mounting. While it was still over a year away, in December 2010 the centennial of the *Titanic* and her tragic sinking was approaching. No ship, liner or otherwise, has garnered more attention, aroused more curiosity, or stimulated more research.

It remains the most enduring sea disaster of all time. The tragedy of a maiden voyage, one that never reached its final destination (New York), had filled countless pages even by 1987, the seventy-fifth anniversary of the sinking – over 300 poems, seventy-five songs, dozens and dozens of books and, even by then, a good number of film and television productions. The year before, her undersea remains were

Sea-going magnificence: the superb first-class smoking room aboard the 882ft-long *Olympic*. (Richard Faber Collection)

Outbound at Southampton in the 1930s. (Cronican-Arroyo Collection)

first located, then photographed and a special video soon produced. First shown in March 1987, it was viewed by a record 4.6 million homes in the United States. Deep interest, near and even full-blown obsession for some, continues to surround the *Titanic*. She is immortal, unlike any other passenger ship, very much in a class by herself.

The *Titanic* was the largest ship afloat in 1912. Launched on 31 May 1911, she was the second of a three-ship set. Her predecessor was a slightly smaller sister ship, the *Olympic*, while the third and final (and possibly least known) member was the *Britannic* (originally to have been called *Gigantic*). The latter ship, larger at over 48,000 tons, never actually completed a passage to New York. When completed in November 1915, she was pressed immediately into military service as a hospital ship, serving the Allies in the First World War. Very sadly, within a year, on 21 November 1916, she was mined by the Germans and sank in the Aegean Sea. Twenty-eight perished.

As Pine Hodges noted:

The 'grand' theme of the *Olympic* & *Titanic* was carried to its apogee on the *Britannic*. Most evident was the First Class Smoking Room, directly inspired by the rival *Aquitania*'s Smoking Room and given a large, central dome as well. The forward Grand Staircase was the first and only one ever fitted with a pipe organ. The forward half of B Deck retained public Promenades, while one port-side suite had a short Private Promenade aft of the staircase. Aft on B Deck, cabins extended

to the ship's side and the A La Carte Restaurant also ran full-beam. Also, while the *Olympic* & *Titanic* had Spartan, utilitarian swimming pools, the *Britannic*'s was highly decorated, inspired by that onboard the *Aquitania*.

In that still-peaceful spring of 1912, however, the *Titanic* stood – at least for a year or so to come – as the world's largest ocean liner and consequently the most publicised. But her owners wanted added distinction, some extra cachet that would draw passengers to fill her 2,603 total berths in the otherwise highly competitive transatlantic trade. Thus, with supposedly 'reinforced steel', she was hailed as the 'world's first unsinkable ship'. Extra watertight compartments were fitted and, as if to almost defiantly test her projected infallibility, she had too few lifeboats and not enough lifesaving gear. Indeed, the public was fascinated, certainly impressed and of course Britain was proud.

At 882ft in length, she was described, in that growing twilight of the Edwardian era, as a 'floating palace'. But, like all other big liners of the time, she was a class-divided palace. There were 905 beds in opulent first class, in top-deck quarters of potted palms and stained-glass skylights, carved wood panels, thick Persian carpets and marble bathtubs. Just below, in somewhat less stylish and less spacious accommodations, there were 564 second-class berths. Further down still, almost in the very bowels of the massive hull, on the very lowest decks and in the very smallest, most spartan spaces, were the third-class passengers, 1,134 of them at maximum. Ironically, and while these third-class travellers paid as little as $10 each

Above Grand gathering: a splendid aerial view at Southampton in the 1920s. The *Olympic* is in the foreground with the *Homeric* and, just behind, Cunard's *Aquitania* is in dry dock. At the bottom right is the *Araguaya* of Royal Mail Lines. (Cronican-Arroyo Collection)

Right Between voyages: the *Olympic* rests between crossings at New York's Pier 59 in a view dated 1931. (Gillespie-Faber Collection)

Excitement: the *Titanic* is seen just prior to launching at Belfast in a view from May 1911. (Albert Wilhelmi Collection)

for the six-night passage to America, where 'the streets were said to be paved in gold', these were in fact the most lucrative, sought-after and most profitable passengers to the *Titanic*'s owners. The greatest steamship profits were made, in fact, from the passengers who were given the least. Those $2,000 suites in first class, occupied by the likes of the Astors, Vanderbilts and titled Europeans, earned far less.

The 23-knot, triple-screw *Titanic* set off from Southampton on 10 April 1912 and, as if a bad omen in itself, she very nearly collided with another liner, the *New York*, as she was undocking. Four days later, just before midnight and in a cold North Atlantic in a position some 380 miles east of Newfoundland, the brand new pride of the British merchant fleet had a far more serious collision. She sideswiped an iceberg that ripped a 300ft-long gash along her starboard side. The cut was soon deemed to be fatal; the ship was doomed. The glitter and glory of the maiden voyage was abruptly turned into tragedy. Two and a half hours later, at precisely 2.20a.m., she sank in 12,000ft of very chilled ocean water. The 'unsinkable ship' was gone from sight. An estimated 1,522 passengers and crew were lost, mostly because of the lack of safety equipment. The first of the speeding rescue ships, Cunard's smallish, 13,500grt *Carpathia*, arrived at the site in a little less than two hours and began receiving the 705 horrified and freezing survivors. This represented a scant 32 per cent of all those who were on board 'the world's safest ship' when it happily departed four days earlier. On the headline-making morning of 15 April, the managers of the White Star Line met with the press outside the company's Lower Manhattan offices. Themselves bewildered, they attempted to assure anxious reporters that 'the *Titanic* did not sink'.

Mrs John Nesbitt, a fellow passenger on a European cruise in the 1990s, recalled:

My aunt and uncle went down on the *Titanic*, but their maid lived. They had gone over to England for Christmas 1911 and took the *Titanic*'s sister ship, the *Olympic*. Typically, they left with lots of luggage and four or five of those bulky, but then essential steamer trunks. They were not due back for six months, until the following summer, but then decided to return earlier, in April. They booked passage on the maiden voyage of what was the world's newest and supposedly grandest liner – and the world's first 'unsinkable' ship!

My aunt especially liked the old White Star Line and its ships. Her journals mention many of their steamers – the *Teutonic*, *Baltic*, *Celtic* and the *Arabic*. She and my uncle felt that White Star had superior ships, service and food compared to the Cunard Line that then sailed on the same route between New York and Liverpool or Southampton.

Evidently, the family maid, who was named Violet, later recalled the sight of that enormous ship slowly sinking, then rising upward into the night sky and then sliding to the bottom. She told us later that my aunt and uncle were quite concerned about her safety and had her placed in one of the earliest lifeboats to leave the drowning liner. But somehow, they themselves stayed too long and the last lifeboats were gone. Violet later worked for my parents and crossed with us in the 1920s and early '30s on such White Star liners as the *Majestic*, *Homeric* and *Laurentic*. She passed away in the early 1940s. But these days, when I travel on modern cruise ships, I still feel a special part of ocean liner history through the tragedy of the *Titanic*.

Numerous inquiries into the *Titanic* sinking followed. The White Star Company itself was never again quite the same and, more dramatically to some onlookers, the tragedy was looked upon as the beginning of the end of the British Empire itself. Smaller, lesser, even odd details were later uncovered as well. There was the survivor who later confessed that she had seen an engine room stoker, thoroughly black with soot, waving and even grinning from the very top of the ship's fourth and only dummy smokestack. The encounter, interpreted as a messenger from the Devil himself, occurred just before the ill-fated liner left her last port of call, Queenstown in southern Ireland. Then there was the tale of the drunken ship's baker, who sat on the very stern rail of the ship and, as it lifted out of the sea to take its final plunge, he slipped off and swam off to safety. This defies the otherwise widely held theory of the enormous suction that such a sinking liner should have created. There is also the case of another crew member who survived the disaster, but then went on to survive the sinking of two other liners, the *Empress of Ireland* in 1914 and the *Lusitania* in 1915.

Perhaps most interesting and intriguing is Morgan Robertson's novel *Futility*. In it, he described – and at great length, in detail and well ahead of the actual technological advances – the creation of the world's largest ocean liner. An exceptionally luxurious ship as well, she too had an extraordinary distinction: she was said to be unsinkable. Then, on the maiden trip (but travelling eastbound) of his 'wonder ship', she was rammed by an iceberg and sank with an enormous loss of life. It too had a shattering effect on world history. His tragedy also occurred on an April night and on a ship called the *Titan*. Amazingly, *Futility* was published in 1898 – fourteen years before the *Titanic* tragedy!

Most of the dead bodies were never recovered from the *Titanic*. The fortunate 705 survivors found their way to lifeboats and safety, and eventually to New York. But many of them, as well as thousands of families of the dead, soon faced another affliction: they had lost their savings, possessions, wage-earners and, in many cases, all three.

The Red Cross and Salvation Army soon mobilised emergency campaigns for the survivors and arranged for short-term housing, clothing and providing small amounts of cash. Other relief agencies soon sprang up in the United States as well as in Great Britain, but all of these were soon exhausted. Ultimately, the sinking of the *Titanic* condemned many surviving families to lifetimes of poverty. Widows and orphans would later beg charitable funds for the likes of a pair of eyeglasses or a set of false teeth.

Annie Mitchell, a New York mother of two whose husband died on the ship, couldn't afford the five-cent subway ride to the relief fund's offices. But the nine-mile walk got her enough cash to care for herself and her children for two months. After that, she was on her own.

The owners of the *Titanic*, a British subsidiary of the American trust controlled by multi-millionaire J.P. Morgan, quickly became tight-lipped after the sinking. When the surviving crew arrived at New York, they were hurriedly hustled back to England on the next ship. They were kept clear of reporters and any official investigators. Even after four months, by July 1912, the White Star Line had paid no claims.

White Star, a firm then valued at $180 million, had the law on its side. Under American federal statute, the company's liability was limited to the value of the property salvaged from the ship (in all, fourteen lifeboats) and its receipts from passenger tickets and cargo. Months later, on 4 October, White Star asked a US Federal Court to certify its liability at a mere $98,000. This was later approved. The ship itself was insured for $5 million.

The White Star Company was later cleared of negligence in inquiries in Washington and London, but both were tainted by political and social prejudice. In London, there was even conclusive evidence that the captain had sailed the ship too fast through iceberg-studded waters, but he was exonerated, as was White Star itself.

By 1913, claims in the United States had risen to $18 million. One passenger, Marion Thayer, asked for $14,190 for her dead husband's luggage, but nothing for his life. Charlotte Cardeza wanted $177,353 for her lost baggage, which included eighty-four pairs of gloves and thirty-three pairs of shoes. Most of the third-class survivors had neither the knowledge nor the means to even hire a lawyer. The surviving crew were in little better financial condition. Their pay stopped when

Sea breezes: strollers are seen along the *Titanic*'s Boat Deck. (Author's Collection)

the ship went down, and they returned to their homes in England with nothing more than the clothes on their backs. Years later, the granddaughter of a first-class steward who was lost claimed, 'With two small children, his widow was given a few sovereigns and that was it. They were left in poverty.'

The most poignant story was that of the families of the musicians on board the *Titanic*, who were playing on deck as the ship went down. Because they were hired by an outside contractor, White Star looked upon them as passengers rather than employees, which meant that their dependents were not entitled to workmen's compensation. A British court later reinforced that contention.

It wasn't until July 1916, more than four years after the *Titanic* sank, that White Star and US plaintiffs came to a settlement. The shipowners agreed to pay $665,000 – or about $430 for each life lost on the *Titanic*.

White Star directors and engineers were concerned about safety in the wake of the *Titanic* sinking. The *Olympic* – as a direct sister ship – was hurriedly given an extended refit in the following winter, in 1912–13. Additional safety measures were installed, including the strengthening of bulkheads, and the adding of lifeboats for her 2,960 passengers and crew. Similar methods of safety were worked into the design and creation of the third of the original trio, the *Gigantic*, soon renamed, rather less pretentiously, as *Britannic*.

By 1987, seventy-five years after her loss, there had been numerous *Titanic* exhibitions, a new round of books and articles, and a special convention staged in Wilmington, Delaware, attended by thousands of members of the Titanic Historical Society. Assuredly, one of the most intriguing topics of the discussion was the then

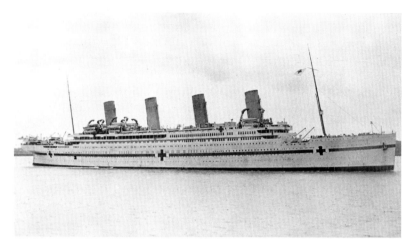

The unfortunate *Britannic*, seen in hospital ship colours, which sailed for only a year. (Alex Duncan)

recently discovered remains of the ship. Over 60,000 photographs were made of the silent vessel in her underwater grave. The stern section, it was uncovered, had broken off and separated, the four funnels were gone and her outer decks were encrusted with inches of sea life. Yet amidst the more fascinating and intriguing details, some of the ship's windows were found to be unbroken, whole whiskey bottles were scattered about on the ocean floor and a chandelier in the main foyer retained a gentle sway even after seventy-five years.

On a windswept, rather chilly Saturday morning a decade later, in April 1997, about fifty of us gathered on the very reduced remains of Pier 54, along Manhattan's West Side. Home for many years to the Cunard Line, most of the terminal's structure was actually pulled down in 1991, but on that spring morning, the pier had a poignant significance: it was the eighty-fifth anniversary of the landing of the survivors of the *Titanic*. Cunard's *Carpathia* had been the heroine and had docked there with the survivors.

Organised by the New Jersey-based Titanic International Society, also present were representatives from Cunard, the BBC, the Red Cross and a cast member from the new Broadway musical *Titanic*. Speakers included *Titanic* expert and author Charles Haas, relatives of victims and even survivors. It was all done with great order, deep respect, honour and a particular thoughtfulness. Each of the speakers was as good as they were informative.

We were told, for example, that the 558ft-long *Carpathia* arrived in New York harbour on the evening of 19 April 1912 to a huge escort – boats listing with the press, great numbers of the curious and, of course, worried families and friends. Immigrant survivors were spared the ordeal of passing through Ellis Island, but instead of going directly to Cunard's Pier 54, the *Carpathia* went instead to Pier 61, White Star's berth almost ten blocks north. Quickly, she landed all *Titanic* crew

members, who were then kept away from all outside contact, namely reporters, and then quickly placed aboard Red Star Line's *Lapland*, which was sailing the next day for Southampton. Afterwards, the *Carpathia* was undocked and moved south to the Cunard pier. But steamship protocol prevailed, even in the darkness of night: the bewildered survivors had to disembark according to class. First-class survivors stepped ashore first followed by second class and then third class. It was midnight before the final *Titanic* passengers were ashore. Later, the White Star Line offered to pay expenses to Cunard, but their Liverpool office very politely and most generously declined.

Anything from the *Titanic* soon became a prized and, decades later, a high-priced collectible. But two of the biggest keepsakes seem to have been neglected and forgotten. The *Carpathia* also landed several *Titanic* lifeboats at Pier 61. These were later sent to a Brooklyn dockyard for refurbishing, but nothing ever came to pass. Left in an open back lot, they eroded over the years, although the wood from one was said to have found its way into a local waterfront saloon.

Months before the anniversary gathering, in November 1996, 1,200 guests crowded into New York City's Neil Simon Theatre for a preview of the tragedy's next reincarnation: a full-blown Broadway musical. Called *Titanic: The Musical*, it eventually opened on 10 April, five days before the eighty-fifth anniversary of the actual sinking. 'The play has been four years in the making,' said award-winning director Peter Stone (his credits including *1776*, *The Will Rogers Follies* and many others). 'The sets will be extraordinary. But there will be no big stars – the *Titanic* will be the star!'

The thirty-one-member cast performed six songs from a specially created score. They dealt with the ship's place in history, immigration to America, the celebratory spirit of the voyage and finally the sinking. Publicity material read:

Rich and poor, young and old, they came from the four corners of the earth: the jewelled and the jaded, the maids and the millionaires, the anonymous and the infamous, the down-at-heel and the upper crust. They travelled faster than man had ever travelled before, surrounded by opulence, captained by a trusted veteran of the high seas and spurred by a tycoon determined to break his own record. Every one of them knew they were bound not just for America, but for history. They were.

By the autumn of 1997, we were off to Broadway to see the musical production. At first, many of us began to yawn – well, at least a little. Following in the wake of countless books and articles and seemingly ceaseless television documentaries, the ever-repeated story of the *Titanic* sinking had opened as an uninteresting, even unappealing Broadway musical. It appeared to be the last venue to retell the story. Could we push ourselves over to a Manhattan theatre and re-watch a story we knew all too well? Of course, even if wearily, many of us did just that.

Well timed and hardly coincidental, the musical actually arrived at a time high on *Titanic* fever. There was a prime-time television mini-series shown the year before, then there were A&E and Discovery Channel documentaries, an interactive CD-Rom called *Titanic: Adventure Out of Time*, yet another book (Hyperion's *Last Dinner on the Titanic*) and, most significantly, James Cameron's $200 million mega-film, the most expensive cinema epic yet. Could a Broadway show squeeze in within all of this?

Indeed it could, and a very pleasant surprise it was. During a Saturday matinee, we sat quite contented, sometimes riveted, eyes and interest fixed. The performances were great, the singers even better. It all flowed. Digital clocks reminded us of the time frame as we 'sailed' westward to tragedy and infamy. The sets were often quite simple, rather basic, but often very clever – two decks, for example, were placed above one another and separated by a thick, black partition. The crow's nest dropped down from the theatre ceiling and, at the end of Act I, a glorious model of the ship itself seemed to sail across a sparkling blue sea. Act II brought us to the tilting, three-storey, hydraulically lifted set. The ship begins to sink, characters start to struggle and finally a mass of furniture (actually, all of it linked to tracks) went crashing to the right (I mean toward the bow). Worthwhile: yes. Recommendable: yes. A new dimension in a somewhat over-told story: yes, again.

Almost at the same time, the remains of the *Titanic* had been the subject of increased research, exploration and even recovery attempts. Attempts to bring a 25ft-long steel section of the hull to the surface failed, however, in the summer of 1996.

If Beatlemania and Psychodelia were buzzwords of the 1960s, *Titanica* was surely one for the late 1990s. Fascination for the ill-fated liner reached inestimable proportions. In some quarters, it was all-out fever, a craze for anything and everything related to the sunken 882ft-long ship. By 1998, eighty-six years after her tragic sinking, her owners could never have imagined that her fame would endure, continue and then reach such a feverish level. James Cameron's film was a huge success – almost anything and everything one might have expected. The film earned hundreds of millions, eventually becoming the very first billion-dollar epic. And even if the on-board romance in the three-and-a-half-hour film was a bit contrived, even reminiscent of soap opera, the sequences of the ship and her actual sinking were pure cinematic magic. The public turned out in huge numbers to see the film: within weeks of opening, the $200 million production costs were well exceeded by over $350 million in ticket sales.

Also in 1998, there were new books in the works, more documentaries, even a rumoured sequel by Cameron. There were also a dozen sites on the World Wide Web, a Swiss rock band called *Panic on the Titanic* and even *Titanic* Ice Beer in Australia. A Las Vegas firm was thinking of a fifty-storey *Titanic* hotel, with the exterior resembling the ship and even capped by four huge funnels. Swiss investors wanted to go a step further and build a modern-day cruise ship version of the *Titanic* and even resurrect the White Star Line name. To counter this, Miami-based Carnival Corporation, by then owners of Cunard and therefore the Cunard-White Star name (the two firms had merged in 1934), quickly put to use a new on-board strategy: White Star Service and, for training purposes, the White Star Academy.

Interest in general tropical cruise bookings was suddenly on the increase, but with added inquiries such as 'will icebergs be seen in the Caribbean?' An exhibit of artefacts taken from the wreckage went on display in Florida and won glowing praise. Aptly, there was yet another big Titanic Historical Society convention in April 1998.

As for the ship itself, there seems, in further examination, to have been very little that went right. She was simply doomed by one error after another. She was going too fast in an ice field, for example, veered away from instead of ramming the berg, had a radio room more interested in celebratory chatter than ice warnings and, while fitted down to the very last silver spoon and brass-polished doorknob, someone forgot binoculars for the crow's nest! Indeed, the sinking of the *Titanic* was more than a sea tale, a tragedy, a massive loss of life, the beginning of the end of an era or the first major blow to the industrial age, but one of the greatest strings and collections of errors and mistakes. A *Titanic* expert noted, 'It is the errors that really intrigue many of us.'

Artefacts from the *Titanic* often command not just large, but huge prices. 'Collecting anything is like expanding your family,' according to retired businessman Stanley Lehrer, and he should know. He has been collecting for well over thirty years and the results are most impressive. Based near New York City, he is a world-class enthusiast-collector, has had a varied career and been immensely successful. He founded and named *USA Today*, for example, and almost became a co-producer of *Titanic*, the Broadway musical. But he is also one of the world's great ocean liner collectors. In fact, he owns the foremost private collection of *Titanic* items. Only

Alive and well! The name *Titanic* often reappears, such as at this used car dealership in Massachusetts. (James Giammatteo Collection)

museum collections are said to be bigger. In 2000, a conservative estimate of the value of Lehrer's collection was in excess of $2 million.

Collecting just about anything came rather late to Stanley Lehrer, however:

In 1969, at my wife's instigation, our family took a cruise, from New York to Nassau. Before that, I'd only been on local ferryboats, going from Brooklyn over to New York and New Jersey. But the magic of the sea and of ships took hold on that first cruise, aboard the liner *Oceanic*. I soon began collecting, beginning with ship menus and deck plans. Later, three men gave me great guidance and pushed me away from general nautical collecting to more specific collecting, to specialisation with the *Titanic*. They were author John Maxtone-Graham, the late Walter Lord (author of the definitive *A Night To Remember*) and the late Ken Schultz. Ken Schultz, that memorabilia dealer extraordinaire, is actually the 'godfather' of my collection as it is today.

Stanley Lehrer's collection grew and grew, and these days it is said to be equal to the collection belonging to no less than the Titanic Historical Society itself. Lehrer's particular passion has been for one-of-a-kind objects from the doomed White Star liner.

I have Molly Brown's talisman, which is in fact the smallest item in my collection, being only three inches tall. I also have a ticket from a weighing machine onboard the *Titanic*. It was found in a box among floating debris after she sank. I have two copies of the very final deck plans of the ship, both dated 29 March 1912. The differences from the previous editions are that all the public rooms are named and the deck chairs are shown by number. One of these plans was, in fact, used by Walter Lord for his early research in the 1950s for his brilliant *A Night To Remember*.

Lehrer's select *Titanic* items also include lots of unpublished photos of the liner, including rare ones from her construction at Belfast, stationery, postcards and an official autograph from Captain Smith, the ship's master. He also has the brass name plate from Lifeboat No.5, a waiter's pad from the first-class grill room and an immigrant examination card used by a third-class passenger. That last item is exceptionally rare, with only seven known to be existence. Such a card would have been pinned to an immigrant's jacket. Another especially cherished item is a letter from a survivor, written on White Star Line letterhead. It is a four-part diagram of the 882ft-long ship's near-collision with another liner, the *New York*, as the *Titanic* departed from Southampton on 10 April 1912 on that otherwise ill-fated maiden voyage. The letter was reportedly worth $30,000 in the buoyant market

Right Another tragedy: Canadian Pacific's *Empress of Ireland* sank following a collision in the St Lawrence River on 28 May 1914. (Author's Collection)

Empress of Ireland, sunk May 29th 1914 930 Lives Lost.

Bringing the dead to Quebec

Storstad after the apalling disaster

of 2000, when anything and everything related to the four-funnel *Titanic* rose to even greater heights. He also has a 6in piece of wood from one of the ship's aft staircases, a square inch of carpet (which once sold for $1,000 a thread), a music book, a butter dish and, as he put it, '300–400 other choice items'.

Long retired, Stanley Lehrer is as busy as ever with the *Titanic* and his collection. He had written, as he called them, nine and a half books on subjects including *Titanic*, but also on such topics as automation, education and a biography of John Dewey. 'That half book,' he added in 2000, 'is for the latest unfinished manuscript.' He also lectures, consults to auction houses, does historic research and often starts new investigations into the mysteries, no matter how slight, of the *Titanic* and her tragic demise. 'I've also became something of a handwriting expert,' he added. 'I found that J. Bruce Ismay's signature, for example, was very often not his, but that of his secretary, who copied it perfectly. Of course, this makes a big difference in valuation.'

Pieces of Lehrer's collection are often loaned out for exhibitions. He often even helps plan the exhibits, works out the details and often personally looks after the well-being of his treasures. 'There is lots to be considered, such as humidity control, security, leasing fees,' he noted. 'It keeps me up all hours, well into the night.'

Lehrer's future is both bright and busy:

> Other *Titanic* collectors and I are planning a major exhibit for 2012 as well as a major book, an A-to-Z catalogue and reference of all *Titanic* artefacts worldwide. In the meantime, I myself continue to collect. I embrace and encourage all other maritime collectors. Most of all, I still believe that even the smallest item is important and that the great beauty of collecting is in the authenticity.

By 2010, the *Titanic* remained at the very peak of ocean liner memorabilia sales. A postcard mailed from Queenstown sold for $43,000, while a menu card from the delivery voyage from Belfast to Southampton fetched $75,000. A handwritten log book of dead bodies brought ashore at Halifax changed hands at a New York City auction for $50,000.

There are also seemingly limitless indirect links to the *Titanic*. In the summer of 2009, for example, a red-brick building located along Manhattan's West Side waterfront and built in 1908 was restored and renovated as the Jane Street Hotel. Located quite close to what was once the Cunard terminal at West 14th Street, the reopening made news and, rather surprisingly, was linked to the *Titanic*. Built originally with 156 rooms (which measured a mere 7ft by 7ft square) for seamen (ordinary seamen paid twenty-five cents a night while it was fifty cents for officers, cooks and stewards), it seems that some 100 survivors from the *Titanic* were sheltered there in April 1912. Some were destitute and concerned, considerate New Yorkers left money and clothes for them. One night, they gathered together for a memorial service at the hotel and offered a roaring chorus of *Nearer, My God, to Thee*.

In April 2012, for the centenary, the cruise ship *Balmoral*, owned by the Fred Olsen Line, has been chartered to recreate the *Titanic*'s westbound passage. With 1,400 berths, it sold out rather quickly. She will cross from Southampton to New York and be positioned exactly on the site of the sinking on 14–15 April. A second cruise, shorter in duration, will depart from New York and all while special exhibitions, displays and lectures will be presented on both sides of the Atlantic. Yet more new, sometimes insightful books are also planned.

There was another noted, documented peacetime disaster involving passenger ships. Canadian Pacific's 15,000grt *Empress of Ireland*, used on the Liverpool–Quebec City route, was off on an eastbound crossing on 28 May 1914. But soon, in thickening fog in the St Lawrence, she collided with a Norwegian freighter, the *Storstad*, which was carrying 10,000 tons of coal to Montreal. Holed in her hull, the *Empress* flooded in less than fifteen minutes, quickly turning over and then promptly sank before her passengers could even get to the upper decks and board the lifeboats. In the wake of the *Titanic* tragedy just two years before, public confidence in passenger ships was shaken, if only momentarily.

3

THE FIRST FRENCH FLOATING PALACES

Collectables! In October 2010, there was a great exhibition of memorabilia from the glorious age of French ocean liners at the Gare Maritime, the grand, pre-war passenger ship terminal at Cherbourg. As the brand new Cunard liner *Queen Elizabeth* came to call for the first time, there was a historical link: some of her Cunard predecessors had berthed there as well: the *Queen Mary*, the original *Queen Elizabeth*, the *Queen Elizabeth 2* and modern-day Cunarders the *Queen Mary 2* and *Queen Victoria*. It was the appropriate setting for an ocean liner exhibition. The collection centred, of course, on French passenger ships, especially those from 'the Transat', the illustrious Compagnie Generale Transatlantique, known simply as the French Line to Americans and many others. There remains the greatest interest in French liners: of course the *Normandie*, that stunning Art Deco dreamboat commissioned in 1935, the decoratively innovative *Ile de France* (from 1927) and the more recent *France*, completed in 1962 and scrapped as recently in 2008. But two of France's earlier Atlantic 'big liners' were also represented: the four-funnel *France* of 1912 and the highly popular *Paris*, first intended for 1915, but then long delayed by the First World War and so not in service until the middle of 1921.

Compared to Cunard and White Star and even the Germans, the French were rather 'slow starters' on the Atlantic circuit. They moved forward rather slowly, almost cautiously, and gained attention in 1891 with the 9,000grt *La Touraine*. A sleek ship often compared to a large yacht, she was known to 'behave splendidly' in rough weather and was the largest liner on the Le Havre–New York run of her time. With her, the French pointedly avoided large size and speed, and instead concentrated on refined, elegant living at sea. Haute cuisine and luxurious suites and first-class accommodation soon became well-recognised features of the French Line. On board, the service was said to be flawless, the cooking supreme.

The company trumpeted its slogan: 'You are in France the moment you cross the gangplank!' Innovatively, it was the French who merged first with second class and created cabin class. *La Touraine* was very successful and was soon followed by the 11,100grt sisters *La Savoie* and *La Lorraine*. They were the first ships to offer suites in first class: lavish quarters with bedrooms, dressing rooms, trunk rooms, sitting rooms and a full bathroom. Parisian directors soon became even more enthusiastic and certainly more progressive.

A new, more expansionist management took over in 1904 and no fewer than seventeen French passenger ships were created between 1905 and 1911. The most important of these was the 13,700grt *La Provence*, completed in 1906 and, having a trial speed of 23 knots, ranked as one of the fastest liners on the North Atlantic. She reached New York in just over six days. But an even bigger, more lavish ship was soon on the drawing boards. Weighing in at 23,600 tons and the first and only French liner to be capped by four funnels, *La Picardie* was the culmination of CGT's first fifty years. She was the ultimate symbol of trans-ocean might, power and prestige. When she slipped down the ways at Chantiers de Penhoet at Saint-Nazaire on a late summer's day in 1910, however, her name had been changed. Seemingly more appropriate, she was christened *France* and soon became the great national maritime symbol. She was France's very own 'floating palace' and inaugurated a succession of some of the most spectacular liners ever built.

As the first steel plates were laid in place at Saint-Nazaire for this new French flagship, the first decade of the new century was drawing to a close. While the size, power and decorative style of passenger liners were expanding, business was booming. Steerage passages were increasing by great numbers. But regular traffic in first as well as second class increased as well. The battle to produce the most luxurious first-class accommodation was as fervent as ever. Every steamer company

Above Early French Line: the *La Touraine*, in a view dated 1900, is seen departing for New York from Le Havre. (Author's Collection)

Below The only four-stacker belonging to the French, the *France* is seen underway in the mid-Atlantic. (French Line)

wanted its share. From her towering fore mast, the Tricolour flew proudly as the 713ft-long *France* went into service in the spring of 1912, just days after the ill-fated *Titanic* plunged to the bottom of the western Atlantic.

The *France* was very quickly established on the Atlantic circuit as a ship of high luxury and great comfort. Of course, her cooking was immediately praised – and often envied. Her first-class quarters were soon favoured by the sea-going social set, those millionaires, aristocrats and even royals who ferried between European and American shores. At New York especially, passengers and visitors alike were reminded that the *France* carried enough lifeboats for her 2,026 passengers (534 first class, 442 second class, 250 third class and 800 steerage). The loss of the larger *Titanic* was still very much in the public mind. Below decks, the quadruple-screw, steam turbine-driven *France* was intended to do as much as 25 knots (24 knots was her official service speed), notably faster than the 21-knot *Titanic*, for example. The *France*'s coal bunkers had a capacity of just over 5,000 tons, allowing for a daily consumption of 680 to 720 tons.

The *France* was soon dubbed 'the Chateau of the Atlantic', primarily because of her superb first-class décor and decoration. Her first-class restaurant was done in very fine Louis XIV style and introduced the prized novelty of a grand staircase as an entrance. Beautifully dressed, bejewelled ladies in particular enjoyed the opportunity of making a stunning entrance, indeed 'the grande descent'. The ultra-elegant Salon Louis XIV was said by many to be the best-decorated room on an Atlantic liner prior to the First World War. It included an ornate ceiling,

gilded columns, a domed skylight, a fireplace at the far end and a large portrait of the Sun King himself. Afterwards, to pass an evening in mid-ocean, first-class travellers might choose the exotic Moorish salon, where they listened to the sounds of a working fountain that played continuously under a thoughtfully selected Algerian fresco.

The *France* upgraded the level of first-class luxuries, from cabine de luxe to cabin grand luxe. Dubbed a 'princely set of rooms', these accommodations could sleep up to six and thereby created a sort of 'glorious isolation' for the rich, very rich and, better still, the titled. Each suite had three canopied beds and two others, complete with elaborate brass headsteads. Each had an Empire-style dining room, a drawing room, full bathroom and adjoining servants' quarters.

The grand traditions of La Belle Epoque of course included grand dining. As an example, at the beginning of every voyage, no fewer than eighteen barrels of pâté de foie gras was loaded aboard the *France*. Over 200 items were listed on a gold-trimmed first-class menu and dinners might run to as many as eight courses.

Right The 34,000grt *Paris* is seen in the big floating dock at the Wilton-Fijenoord shipyard at Schiedam in Holland. The dock could handle ships up to 46,000 tons. (Richard Faber Collection)

Opposite above Poetic scene: the *France* arrives off the breakwater at Le Havre. (Richard Faber Collection)

Opposite below Outbound from New York on a cruise, the *France* is seen here in the latter years of her career. (Cronican-Arroyo Collection)

Early morning: the very popular *Paris* approaches New York harbour in 1929, ending a westbound crossing from Le Havre and Plymouth. (Cronican-Arroyo Collection)

Manhattan Docks: the *Paris* (right) is together with the older *France* (left) in this scene at Pier 57, at the foot of West 14th Street. (French Line)

'The *France* was a true "castle on the Atlantic",' commented John Malcolm Brinnin, author of the insightful *The Sway of the Grand Saloon*. 'She made inroads on Anglo-German supremacy. She had charm, chic and a tapestried ambience that appealed to passengers who preferred haute cuisine over grandiosity and high speed.' Like other liners, the *France* had her odd blemish. One passenger reported, 'She rolled like a sick headache'.

Called to duty, the *France* was used first as a hospital ship and then as a troopship during the war years before resuming commercial service in 1919. She served,

although increasingly dated, until 1932 and then sat idle for nearly three years before going to shipbreakers at Dunkirk.

As both catalyst and benefactor, the French Government wanted more, a bigger share, of the lucrative Atlantic passenger trade. National prestige was also important – 'the glory of France' had to be proudly represented on the most important sea route in the world: the North Atlantic to America. Assuredly, the French anxiously wanted to join the British and the Germans in that elite pocket of ocean liner supremacy. To support this, the French Government created a new mail and subsidy agreement, one that called for four large liners, perhaps even one every four years.

The next step upward was the 34,500grt *Paris*, whose construction was begun in 1913, but then ground to a silent halt a year later as the war started. She was, in fact, very quietly, almost unceremoniously, launched in September 1916, but then the unfinished, 764ft-long hull was shunted off to an anchorage to await the end of hostilities. When she finally emerged in the summer of 1921, the French could not have been more pleased or proud.

The *Paris* had great speed, luxurious innards and a very definite style and personality, two elements not created in a shipyard. Once in service, in the 1920s, she was almost without equal on the Atlantic. She was also immensely popular and profitable. Year after year, she crossed between Le Havre and New York with the lowest percentage of empty berths.

The smart-looking *Paris* differed from the earlier *France*. On the outside, she had three, well-grouped funnels instead of four. Within, the gilded Louis XIV gave way to a more innovative art nouveau, even a primitive Art Deco. Her interiors were soon judged by New York reporters as 'new generation'. One description of her accommodations included:

> The Promenade Deck is enclosed with glass screens for the whole of its length. It is also rubber tiled to reduce sound and prevent slipping. On this deck is the Main Smoking Room and the Salon de The, where 'moderne' is the style and which is supplemented by light colored walls, indirect lighting and a large skylight. In the center of this room is one of the finest achievements of the Paris's decoration, namely the illuminated dance floor. Frosted glass panels in the actual floor are illuminated from beneath by lights, giving a very pleasing effect. The Grand Salon is done in the style of Marie Antoinette, yet in a modern way. It has a large dome, the topmost part of which is glass, as well as large windows and mirrors. The first-class main dining room included a large stairway leading to the Balcony Dining Room. The room itself was supported by square pillars, over which a large glass dome formed a central nave with an aisle on each side, both upstairs and downstairs. Halfway up the staircase at each end of the room was an array of magnificent mirrors that reflected both the light and the colors of this wonderful room.

The immensely popular *Paris* endured, but only to burn and then capsize at her Le Havre berth in April 1939. Subsequent salvage was postponed due to the Second World War, but then there were further damages to her sunken, scorched remains during heavy bombings in 1944. She was finally declared a menace in 1947 and quickly broken up where she lay.

Powered by steam turbines, with four screws and capable of 22 knots, here we see a part of the engine room of the 764ft *Paris*. She was the largest and finest French liner of her day. (French Line)

Destruction: following a fire at her Le Havre berth in April 1939, the beautiful *Paris* capsized and was a complete loss. (Richard Faber Collection)

4

COLOSSUS: GIANT GERMAN THREESOME

Germanic prestige! The German cruise ship *Europa* was voted, by at least one very reliable, well-respected source, as the finest passenger ship afloat in 2010. Indeed, it was a great honour, the highest accolade, for that 29,000grt ship that carries as few as 400 guests in ultra-luxurious quarters. German tradition of luxuries, fine appointments and superb service and food, have been a long tradition. Alone, it covers well over 100 years – from the gilded age of such Atlantic speed queens as the four-funnel *Kaiser Wilhelm der Grosse* to even greater behemoths such as the *Imperator* and *Vaterland*.

A century ago, in the age of intense maritime (as well as political and military rivalries) between Imperial Britain and Imperial Germany, the biggest ocean liner yet was launched. She flew the German flag. Named by the Kaiser himself, on 23 May 1912 (and just five weeks after the tragic sinking of the British *Titanic*), she was christened at a Hamburg shipyard as the appropriately named *Imperator*. (The name *Europa* was first considered, by the way.) But while far from complete or even completely measured and sized, she was already dubbed the 'colossus of the Atlantic'.

A little more than four years before, at the end of 1907, there were seven four-stackers, all of them ocean giants, in North Atlantic passenger service: the North German Lloyd's *Kaiser Wilhelm der Grosse*, *Kronprinz Wilhelm*, *Kaiser Wilhelm II* and, finally, the *Kronprinzessin Cecilie*, Hamburg America Line's *Deutschland* and, flying the Red Ensign for Britain, Cunard's *Lusitania* and *Mauretania*. The overwhelming success (and great profitability) of almost all of these ships (the mechanically troubled, disappointing *Deutschland* was the most obvious single exception) led almost immediately to plans for even bigger, grander creations. Cunard, for example, began thinking of a third ship while White Star Line planned for nothing less than a grandiose trio. But it was the Germans, in the form

of the mighty Hamburg America Line, that would pull out all the stops and begin to plan for a threesome of successively larger superliners that would easily surpass all others. If the *Lusitania* and *Mauretania* at 31,000 tons each were the biggest liners afloat in 1907, the new Germans, so it was estimated, would exceed the almost unimaginable 50,000-ton mark.

Hamburg America selected a three-funnel design for their giant liners, however. On board the *Imperator*, rising 69ft above the upper deck, these stacks were among the tallest ever fitted to a liner. Along the 919ft-long liner's decks were no less than eighty-three lifeboats and twin motor launches (equipment prompted by the very recent *Titanic* sinking). There were four four-bladed propellers that could make 185 revolutions per minute and twin engine rooms that were 95ft and 69ft long. The massive bunkers could hold 8,500 tons of coal. As the biggest ship of any kind yet created, the 52,117grt *Imperator* was truly symbolic of Imperial Germany's heightened technological might. The Kaiser himself was more than pleased; the British deeply jealous.

The 23-knot *Imperator* was completed in the spring of 1913. She left Cuxhaven (near Hamburg) on her maiden crossing to New York (actually, the Hamburg America terminal was across the Hudson in Hoboken, New Jersey) via Southampton and Cherbourg. The otherwise joyous, festive trip was marked, however, by one serious and worrisome blemish: the mighty *Imperator* was extremely top-heavy and – great horrors – even seen to be often listing. 'She was a ship of gloomy panelled majesty,' said John Malcolm-Brinnin. 'She was hard to handle, clumsy, totally Teutonic. She was a creation of industry without any pretensions to beauty.'

Along with her soaring masts, three mustard-coloured funnels and seemingly endless lifeboats, even the slightest beauty of the giant *Imperator* was lessened by the fitting of a rather grotesque figurehead affixed to the bow. Useless and even senseless, this piece of added ocean liner architecture pushed up the length of the ship and so guaranteed her position as world's largest as well as longest ship. The figurehead amounted to a bland-eyed eagle wearing a reduced crown on its otherwise snakelike head. Its cast-iron claws gripped a cast-iron globe, which itself was fastened to a cast-iron sunburst of flared golden spikes. It was embossed with the Hamburg America Line motto: *Mein Feld Ist die Welt*. In all, it uncharmingly added to the bulkiness of the ship itself. It was short-lived, however, and to many, quite happily. On her third voyage, in stormy seas, the entire imperial eagle and globe were ripped from the bow and sank into the sea below. But the *Imperator* had that other, far more serious problem: she was top heavy. In rough seas, she rolled and listed so seriously as to terrify not only passengers, but the crew alike. Hamburg America engineers quickly decided on some drastic modifications. First, truckloads of ponderously heavy furniture, all of it ornamental, were removed. Afterwards, even the big marble baths in the first-class suites went and then the marble and mahogany fixtures in the Continental Grill were gone. For the latter, a Winter Garden was created with lightweight cane furniture. But all this wasn't quite enough. Each of the three towering funnels had to be reduced in height by 9ft. Finally, and an almost added indignity and humiliation, 2,000 tons of concrete were poured into her bottom to improve stability.

The *Imperator* was a 'floating city', designed to carry more passengers than any other liner afloat, 4,594 in all. These were arranged between 908 in first class, 972 in second class, 942 in third class and 1,772 in steerage. Ignoring the possibilities of a future military conflict, the directors of the Hamburg America Line saw only the best times ahead. The number of first-class transatlantic travellers was increasing and European immigration to American shores was equally as promising (alone, nearly 1 million crossed to New York between January and August 1914). The *Imperator* and her two projected near-sisters were expected to profit greatly from this prosperity.

'The *Imperator* was intended to surpass the *Olympic*-class ships as well as the *Aquitania* and at all levels,' observed Pine Hodges:

> Her no-nonsense exterior profile was meant to impress by virtue of its sheer massiveness. Meanwhile, her eighteenth-century, French-style interiors were carried to even greater heights. Most impressive perhaps was the Romanesque Pompeian Bath, a double-height swimming pool that was actually an extravaganza, complete with its own Grand Staircase. Equally stunning rooms up on the Promenade Deck were the enormous Social Hall and the Ritz-Carlton Restaurant, both fully double-height spaces in which passengers were comfortably grouped together congenially upon plush furnishings. The Ritz-Carlton Restaurant combined the *Olympic*'s earlier Palm Courts and A La Carte Restaurant into one combined, impressively staged affair, literally in the centre of the Promenade Deck. The *Imperator* was also the first liner to place lifeboats in bays two decks lower in the ship's side, a design practice that is almost universal in today's cruise ships.

The mighty 52,117grt *Imperator*, then the world's largest ship of any kind, arrives in New York's Upper Bay. (Cronican-Arroyo Collection)

Slightly longer, a bit bigger and, happily, somewhat better looking on the outside than her previous near-sister, the 54,282grt *Vaterland* was commissioned in April 1914, just months before the dramatically unexpected outbreak of the First World War in high summer. She became the biggest ship afloat. A better sea boat than the *Imperator* and temporarily the new national flagship, she was not without her critics, however. 'She is nothing more than an over-decorated hostelry disguised as an ocean liner,' wrote an Atlantic liner pundit. Others were more generous, even kindly. Pine Hodges noted that the ship did have some notations and innovations. 'The *Vaterland* was the first liner to employ divided uptakes, allowing a "Grand Enfilade", based on the Versailles concept of one room leading into another, without uptakes or any other obstructions blocking the way.'

But amidst the festivity, even fanfare, of the maiden season for the new *Vaterland*, there were increasing deep worries for the Germans. Within months, as the Germans declared war on most of Europe, Hamburg America decided to leave the 950ft-long ship in a 'neutral haven', at her 2nd Street berth in Hoboken. She would sit there, in the confines of New York harbour, for three long years, but then only to be seized by the US Government, in April 1917, and then used to carry troops that would fight against the very nation that created her. That September, after repairs, she was given a new name: USS *Leviathan*. She was the largest Allied troop transport.

S. S. BERENGARIA   -   Pompeian Swimming Pool   -   CUNARD LINE

Opposite; clockwise from far left
Styled after a Bavarian hunting lodge, the splendid smoking room aboard the four-class *Imperator*. (Hapag-Lloyd)

Grand style: the extraordinary Pompeian indoor swimming pool aboard the *Imperator*, but seen in this view from her later days as Cunard's *Berengaria*. (Richard Faber Collection)

Happy passengers: dancing in the first-class main hall aboard the 4,594-passenger *Imperator*. (Hapag-Lloyd)

Austere and basic: a four-bunk cabin in the lower-deck steerage quarters aboard the *Imperator*. It cost approximately $10 for the week-long passage to America and to a New Life. (Hapag-Lloyd)

Reassurance: the *Imperator* had a commodore as well as four staff captains. (Hapag-Lloyd)

Safety first: in the wake of the *Titanic* disaster, safety precautions including frequent boat drills were enforced aboard the new *Imperator* in 1913. (Hapag Lloyd)

Clockwise from right
Immigrant children pose in this view from 1913. (Hapag-Lloyd)

Outbound at New York, the bow of the 919ft-long *Imperator* is headed south, bound for another crossing to Europe. The sixty-storey Woolworth Building, then the world's tallest skyscraper, is to the left while the forty-seven-storey Singer Building is in the centre. On end, the 919ft-long *Imperator* would be taller than the 790ft-high Woolworth tower. (Hapag-Lloyd)

The great eagle and globe aboard the *Imperator*. (Cronican-Arroyo Collection)

Right, from top
Festive occasion: the launching of the 950ft-long *Vaterland* at the Blohm & Voss Shipyard at Hamburg. The date is 3 April 1913. (Albert Wilhelmi Collection)

Preparation: the 54,282grt *Vaterland* is being readied, at the Blohm & Voss yard, for her formal commissioning in this scene from March 1914. (Albert Wilhelmi Collection)

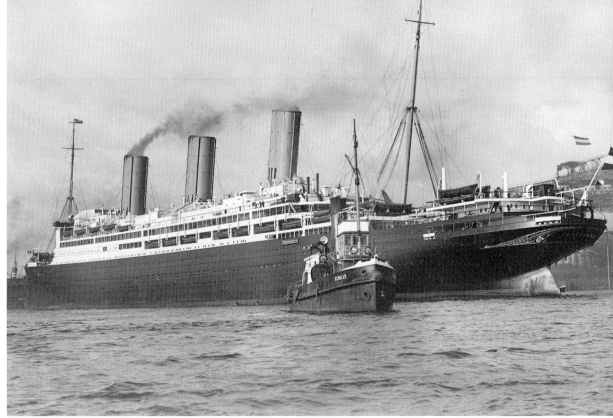

The last of Hamburg America's 'Big Three', the 56,551grt *Bismarck* goes down the ways at Blohm & Voss on 20 June 1914. Work on the new liner would cease in less than two months, however, as the First World War erupted. (Hapag-Lloyd)

5

THE SHIP BEAUTIFUL: THE SPLENDID *AQUITANIA*

Mediterranean bound! In the autumn of 2010, I was honoured to be a guest speaker aboard the second voyage, part of the maiden season, of Cunard's brand new 92,000grt *Queen Elizabeth*. A most splendid ship, her interiors were contemporary, very comfortable and all done with strong suggestion and influence of the evocative 1930s, another grand Art Deco liner era. Most successfully, she evokes Cunard's rich and colourful history. She is a grand reminder, a reflection of glamorous days on great ships in times past. No company, it has been said often, carried more people across the Atlantic: countless tourists, masses of immigrants, millions of troops and, of course, a near continual parade of those Hollywood film stars. Hugely successful, Cunard has created some of the world's greatest, most successful and highly popular liners. The beautiful *Aquitania* is an 'immortal' of twentieth-century ocean liner history and is a direct antecedent of ships such as the new, 2,200-bed *Queen Elizabeth*. In my lectures aboard that newest Cunarder, I mentioned the *Aquitania* on several occasions. One of the most successful liners ever, she remains in strong and vivid memory.

The 45,600grt *Aquitania* was often said to be the most handsome of all the four-stackers (there were fourteen in all). Even to this day, a century later, her romantic-sounding name (after the ancient province in south-west France) conveys the image of a mighty, romantic ocean liner. The 901ft-long ship was long and almost slender, with that quartet of well-balanced funnels (all of which worked, unlike many other three and four-funnel ships with added 'dummy' stacks) and all balanced by an eye-pleasing counter stern.

She was ordered from John Brown & Co., Clydeside builders who had also created the great *Lusitania* several years earlier. The order was signed in December 1910, just as Belfast shipbuilders were finishing the *Olympic* and preparing the *Titanic*, and as the Germans, across the North Sea at Hamburg, were planning for their giant *Imperator*, *Vaterland* and then, biggest of all, the *Bismarck*. The great ocean liner continued and at a higher pitch. The *Aquitania* was designed under strict Admiralty supervision. Although the war was still over three years off, the idea that such a large liner might be used as an armed merchant cruiser was very much in the thinking and planning down in London, at Admiralty House. The general Cunard plan was that she would complement the *Lusitania* and *Mauretania*, creating a three-ship express service between Liverpool and New York. With the Blue Riband

Prepared for launching, the 901ft-long *Aquitania* rests on the ways at the John Brown & Co. Ltd shipyard at Clydebank in Scotland. The date is April 1913. (Albert Wilhelmi Collection)

Summer sailing: the *Aquitania* is making a midday departure from New York's Pier 54
in this scene from the 1920s. (Richard K. Morse Collection)

Fine dining on the high seas: the splendid first-class restaurant aboard the *Aquitania*. (Richard Faber Collection)

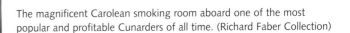

The magnificent Carolean smoking room aboard one of the most popular and profitable Cunarders of all time. (Richard Faber Collection)

But for more select and intimate dining, first-class passengers had the option of a grill room. (Richard Faber Collection)

Above Busy day: Southampton in the 1920s – with the *Homeric* and then the *Olympic* on the left; the *Aquitania* and then the *Berengaria* to the right. (Cunard Line)

Right Heavy seas! In a scene dated 11 March 1936, the *Aquitania* is seen from the French liner *Ile de France*. The two liners were steaming side by side, both bound for New York. (Richard Faber Collection)

securely belonging to the very powerful *Mauretania*, there was absolutely no intention that this new ship should compete in the Atlantic speed race.

Launched on 21 April 1913 (and just as the mighty *Imperator* was coming into service), she left Clydebank thirteen months later, in May, for three days of sea trials. At top speed, she reached 24 knots, a full knot more than John Brown and Cunard engineers had expected.

Equally beautiful on the inside, the 3,230-berth *Aquitania* was quickly appraised as the best decorated ship in the Cunard Line fleet. 'Cunard seemed to throw away the book in fitting out a sea-going museum that would offer a retrospective exhibition of European culture,' wrote John Malcolm-Brinnin. The first-class restaurant was done in Louis XVI style, giving the appearance more of a room in a chateau than in an ocean liner. The Jacobean smoking room was copied from part

With the port's mighty floating, heavy-lift crane on the left, the *Aquitania* rests between crossings in Southampton's Ocean Dock in this view dated 1935. (Frank O. Braynard Collection)

of the Greenwich Hospital and the Palladian lounge had its own columns and rose two decks in height.

Even in later years, she held her own. The late Everett Viez visited the *Aquitania* at New York in the late 1920s and during the '30s, and also sailed aboard her, on a short summertime cruise. 'By then, she was the last of the Atlantic four-stackers,' he said. 'She was also possibly the most beautiful of them, both inside as well as out.' From almost the start of her days, she was very fondly dubbed 'the Ship Beautiful'.

She left Liverpool on 30 May 1914 on her maiden voyage to New York, but her commercial life was all too brief. By August, she was promptly requisitioned by the Admiralty for use as an armed merchant cruiser. That role was short-lived, however, when after a serious collision, large ships were seen to be far too risky and better suited as troopships and for doing hospital duties, with military escorts of course. By the spring of 1915, the disguised *Aquitania* had been dispatched to the Dardanelles with troops.

CUNARD

Europe-America

Doppelschrauben-Postdampfer „Amerika"

F. 1023

MÜHLMEISTER & JOHLER, HAMBURG · Dru 242

Hamburg-Amerika
Linie

An Bord
des Dampfers „CLEVELAND"

N° 898   N° 988   MÜHLMEISTER & JOHLER, HAMBURG. DEP.2800   F. 1023

GREAT WESTERN RAILWAY

G.W.R. TENDERS
FETCH & CARRY
PASSENGERS
Baggage & Mails

PLYMOUTH   FISHGUARD

MEETING THE BIG SHIPS

Above Convenient train connections to Cunarders at Plymouth and Fishguard. (Author's Collection)

From far left
To America: the great *Aquitania* is depicted against the famed New York City skyline. (Author's Collection)

When completed in 1905, the 22,225grt, 700ft-long *Amerika* of Hamburg-America Line ranked as the largest liner afloat. (Author's Collection)

Another Hamburg America liner, the *Cleveland*, which divided her time between Atlantic crossings and long cruises. (Author's Collection)

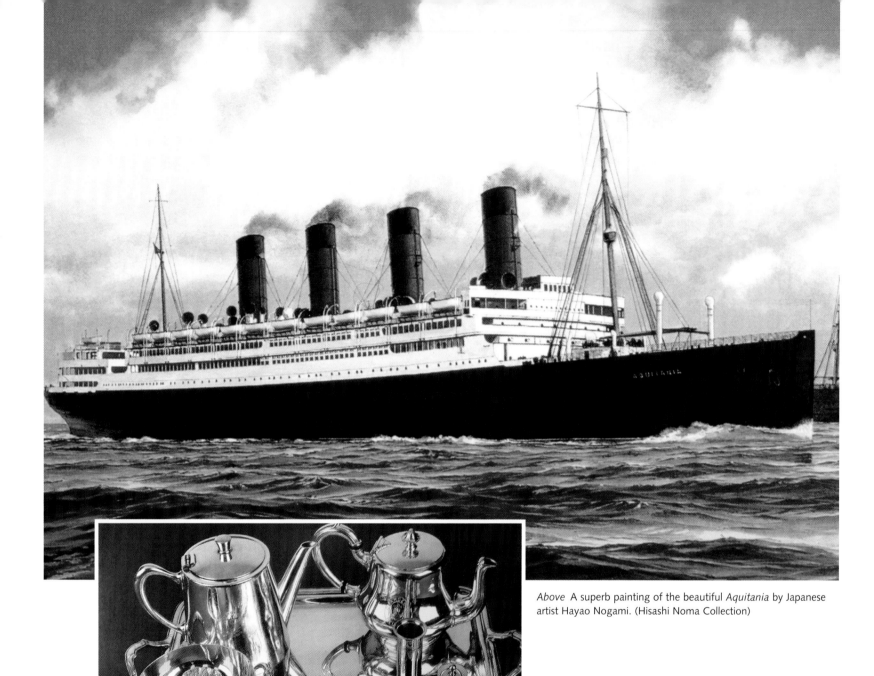

Above A superb painting of the beautiful *Aquitania* by Japanese artist Hayao Nogami. (Hisashi Noma Collection)

Left Fine silverware from the *Lutetia*, built in 1913 for France's Compagnie Sud-Atlantique. (Author's Collection)

Power and strength: the exceptional *Imperator* is superbly depicted in this advertising art of 1913. (Hapag-Lloyd)

Royal Mail Lines' *Atlantis* became, in the 1930s, a very popular cruise ship. Repainted
in all-white, she is depicted here during a summer cruise to the Norwegian fjords.
(Author's Collection)

The *Virginian* of 1905 finished her days, after a fifty-year career, as the *Homeland* of the Home Lines. (James Sesta Collection)

Germanic in tone, the former Hamburg America-North German Lloyd docks in Hoboken, New Jersey. Built in 1905, they are seen here in a view dating from 1983. (Author's Collection)

Above Pier B, at the foot of Third Street in Hoboken, was the last remaining 'finger pier' in Hoboken from the earlier German liner period. The 900ft-long pier collapsed in 1990 and the remains had to demolished. (Author's Collection)

FASTEST STEAMERS IN THE WORLD.

CUNARD LINE

The *Mauretania* and her near-sister, the *Lusitania*, were heavily advertised in their time as the 'fastest steamers in the world'. (Author's Collection)

Opposite Demolition amongst the final remains of the German liner piers in a view from the summer of 1988. (Author's Collection)

The Antwerp-based Red Star Line promoted their service to Canada. (Author's Collection)

French artist Olivier Fischer created this depiction in the 1990s of the four-funnel *France* of 1912. (Author's Collection)

ORIENT CRUISES
NORWAY

13 DAYS for 20 GUINEAS
ANDERSON, GREEN & C° L°, 5, Fenchurch Avenue, LONDON, E.C.3

Red Star Line
Antwerp - Dover - New York

The Red Star Line had a popular service between Antwerp and New York. (Author's Collection)

Similar to P&O, London-based Orient Line offered occasional cruises, including summertime trips to Norway and the Northern Capitals. (Author's Collection)

Above Holland America Line was the premier Dutch shipping company in North Atlantic liner service. (Author's Collection)

From left to right
In addition to their transatlantic services, North German Lloyd offered passenger links from Europe via Suez to Australia as well as the Far East. (Author's Collection)

Cunard's express service between Liverpool (and later Southampton) to New York was unquestionably the company's most important and profitable service. (Author's Collection)

Britain's Union-Castle Line was the dominant passenger line to ports in South Africa. (Author's Collection)

AMERICA
WORLD RENOWNED SERVICES
EUROPE

AQUITANIA

CUNARD LINE

UNION-CASTLE LINE

List
of
Passengers.

Above The splendid *Belgenland* of the Red Star Line. Later a very popular cruise ship, she made seven around-the-world cruises between 1924 and 1930. (Author's Collection)

CIe GLe TRANSATLANTIQUE ◆ FRENCH LINE

PARIS ◆ HÂVRE ◆ NEW·YORK

Albert Sebille was one of France's finest artists and often he created poster and advertising art for the French Line, the Compagnie Generale Transatlantique. (Author's Collection)

Opposite, below left Germany's Hamburg-Sud, the Hamburg-South American Line, created a large passenger fleet for the service between Europe and the East Coast of South America. (Author's Collection)

Opposite, below right Blue Funnel Line, with strong interests in the trades between the UK, Australia and the Far East, was well known for its vivid funnel colouring. The steamer *Nestor*, commissioned in 1913, had one of the tallest funnels to put to sea. (Author's Collection)

The *Giuseppe Verdi* of Italy's Transatlantica Italiana is festively depicted in this scene at Genoa. (Albert Wilhelmi Collection)

Another Transatlantica Italiana passenger ship, the *Dante Alighieri*, is seen here in another departure scene at Genoa. (Albert Wilhelmi Collection)

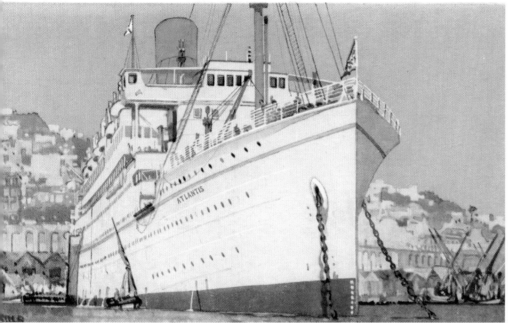

Another view of Royal Mail Lines' classic cruise ship *Atlantis*. Offering periodic Mediterranean cruises, she is shown here at Algiers. (Albert Wilhelmi Collection)

Promoting its service from Britain to South America, the 12,000grt *Asturias* is seen in a comparison to a classic sailing ship. (Albert Wilhelmi Collection)

ORIENT LINE. S.S. "ORMUZ"
14167 TONS.

Summer holiday voyages: Orient Line's *Ormuz* is shown at anchor in Norway's
Geirangerfjord. (Albert Wilhelmi Collection)

Piercing the seas, Royal Mail's *Araguaya* is seen, in fierce determination, bound for the likes of Rio, Santos, Montevideo and Buenos Aires. (Albert Wilhelmi Collection)

6

LONG VOYAGES: OFF TO THE COLONIES & DISTANT OUTPOSTS

Swaying palms and exotic nights! On a balmy evening in March 2010, we departed from Mumbai, sailing off – and under star-filled skies – aboard a glamorous, creature-comfortable, six-star cruise ship. Impeccable in immaculate, glossy white paint and glittering in lights, the ship was off, the great floating hotel underway on a two-week cruise to Middle Eastern ports in Oman, Kuwait, Abu Dhabi, Dubai and, rather unusually, Iran. It was all pure pleasure – idyllic and indulgent days on board a modern-day moving palace; tours and wanderings ashore, visiting temples and ruins and the inevitable gift shops. At times, it was also reflective, even historic, hinting of romantic, long-ago days and languid nights of steamers plying exotic routes, carrying multi-classed passengers, well loaded with crated supplies and bags of mail, and trading between and often connecting and interconnecting the great political and trading empires. Much has changed today, of course, with cityscapes of soaring clusters of steel and glass skyscrapers, luxury residential towers and increasing evidence of more laptops and mobile phones than straw baskets and wheeled wooden carts. Mumbai – or Bombay as it was then – was one of the great outposts for shipping. Sturdy, all-black-funnelled P&O passenger ships, for example, were always in the harbour, appearing on their well-timed, three and four-week runs down from London. High commissioners and civil servants, traders and teachers, the engineers and the clergy and the occasional Indian, even a bejewelled maharaja and his entourage, might be aboard. In the cargo holds would be British-manufactured goods (from woollen goods and whiskies to steam locomotives and heavy-duty machinery), indeed the home products; the return trips would include the likes of Indian spices, textiles and, of course, teas.

In 1910, the Strait of Gibraltar was one of the busiest shipping routes, and especially for passenger ships, in the world. Ships were heading off, or returning, on long-haul voyages – such as Liverpool to Singapore and Hong Kong, London to Mombasa and Sydney, Hamburg to Yokohama and Shanghai, Amsterdam to Batavia and Bangkok, and Marseilles to Saigon and Papeete. Passenger ships on these routes, however, were mostly combination in purpose: passengers as well as freight (including the all-important mails and therefore lucrative government subsidies and operating contracts). They tended to be smaller (often under 10,000 tons), moderately, even modestly decorated and comparatively slow (some round voyages took as long as nine to ten months). These ships, while quite important in their time and for their purpose, have comparatively received far less attention and documentation than, say, the big, grand Atlantic liners. Passengers, whether in some comfort in upper-deck first class or in cramped, lower-deck third class, were travelling mostly for necessity. Yes, there might, on occasion, be the odd eccentric tourist, perhaps under the watchful eye of a guide and bound for, say, the ruins of ancient Egypt or the mountainous temples of exotic India. But quite simply, most passengers endured a long voyage because they had to. For overseas travel, steamers were the only way to go.

On long, often warm voyages, wood-panelled lounges and writing rooms and shaded deckchairs under canvas tarps were filled with a great cast of shipboard characters: planters, brokers, traders, administrators, archaeologists, adventurers, missionaries, even animal hunters. Shipboard meals were often long, drawn-out affairs, less about epicurean delights than simply passing time, while daytime was dotted with very little to do other than morning deck games and a long afternoon nap. Evenings were more about conversation or a good book in a quiet lounge or, on somewhat larger ships, perhaps dancing twice a week. But these voyages, while long and slow, had a certain appeal, even a special glamour, as well. They were often part of great adventures too.

P&O's 605ft-long *Naldera* and her near-sister *Narkunda* were two of that company's prime passenger ships on the runs to Bombay and to Melbourne and Sydney. Delayed by the war, they were finally commissioned in 1920. (V.H. Young & L.A. Sawyer Collection)

Another P&O liner, the 600-passenger *Mantua*, dating from 1909, was used on the London–Suez–Sydney service as well as for periodic cruises. (Alex Duncan)

On the Eastern routes through Suez, the first port was often Port Said, where passengers usually went ashore to buy inexpensive souvenirs. Passage through the canal itself might take several days, warm and possibly monotonous and interrupted perhaps by a blowing sandstorm. The Red Sea was usually ferociously hot, the rising midday temperatures almost insufferable. Water was generously passed around to travellers, who in an almost groggy state often laid about in canvas deckchairs. At night, passengers usually abandoned their steamy cabins for a chair along the open promenade or sought a good night's sleep in a place on the teak decks, under endless Eastern stars. At Aden, also in blistering heat, there was the brief diversion of watching 'copper-skinned beggar children' diving from open boats for coins. The breezes of the open sea in the Indian Ocean might offer some relief, with some ships now changing course and heading for ports such as Bombay while others steamed much farther east. Colombo or Ceylon might be the next stopover, and a brief diversion, before ships might head for Australia or northward to Calcutta and Rangoon or across the Strait of Malacca to Singapore. The Dutch ships went on to Batavia while the French ones were charted to colonial Vietnam. The longest voyages went farther, heading along the grey waters of the China Sea for Hong Kong, China and Japan.

Migration supported passenger ships on these distant, long-haul routes as well. It was, in fact, a major business. Between 1911 and 1913, for example, some 200,000 Brits left home shores for new lives in Australia. Another 300,000 went elsewhere in the otherwise vast British Empire. Especially on the long route out to Australia, migration figured so heavily in passenger ship operations that some vessels only offered low-fare, third-class quarters. These austere accommodations were always heavily booked.

P&O's very strong, vast services to Australian ports, to Fremantle, Melbourne and Sydney, were dominated by the new 12,400-ton sisters *Maloja* and *Medina*. The latter ship actually went on to great notation after she was selected to serve as a big royal yacht between November 1911 and May 1912. Refitted and repainted in all-white, she carried Britain's King George V and Queen Mary and their entourages out to India, for the grand Delhi Durbar. An extravaganza of hugely theatrical proportions, it was all staged as a reaffirmation of Empire, the sheer destiny of the British to rule over 'less fortunate' others. Also, P&O reinforced its prime colonial service, between London and Bombay, in 1914 with the 11,500-ton *Kaisar-I-Hind* and then planned even larger ships, at nearly 16,000 tons each. But these three-funnel sisters, the *Naldera* and *Narkunda*, were delayed by the war and not commissioned until 1920. P&O also looked especially to the low-fare, migrant trade and so created a set of five sisters – the *Ballarat, Beltana, Benalla, Berrima* and *Borda* – between 1911 and 1913. With large cargo capacities as well, the all-third-class passenger spaces were quite basic, with large dormitories, and had up to 1,100 berths each. They would make eight-week voyages out from London to Fremantle, Melbourne and Sydney, but then return home primarily as freighters. With the link to Britain as strong as ever, business boomed. Also London-

Orient Line's *Orvieto*, a ship from 1909 and used on the UK–Australia route, is rather oddly depicted by an artist in 'stormy weather' and was noted to be a 'keepsake of a voyage'. (Albert Wilhelmi Collection)

headquartered, the Orient Line added no less than six 12,000-tonners, beginning in 1908 and a set finally finished in 1911. They were the *Orsova, Otway, Osterley, Otranto, Orvieto* and *Orama*. There was even a seventh ship, the *Ormonde*, added in 1919. Another British shipowner, the Shaw Savill Line, commissioned the 18,500-ton, 679ft-long *Ceramic* for their Liverpool–Suez–Melbourne–Sydney service beginning in 1913. Carrying up to 600 all-third-class passengers, she ranked as the largest liner in Australian service of her day. Smaller firms such as the Aberdeen Line, based in Scotland, added a trio of 11,000-tonners: the *Pericles, Themistocles* and *Demosthenes*. Again, each ship carried the greater number of passengers down in third class. Liverpool's Blue Funnel Line added their largest passenger ships to date as well, 10,000-ton combination passenger-cargo vessels, the *Aeneas, Ascanius* and *Anchises*, for the UK–Australia trade. Each ship carried 288 passengers, but all of them in first-class quarters. They aimed at general passenger business, namely the business and governmental trades. Very successful, they were followed in 1912–13 by the 14,500-ton sisters *Nestor* and *Ulysses*. Both had increased accommodations, for up to 350 all-first-class passengers each. Clever shipowners Blue Funnel invested in the immigrant trade as well, adding the *Talthybius* and *Ixion*, which carried 600 all-third-class passengers.

European colonial trades included the great links of France's Messageries Maritimes. Based at Marseilles, their large fleet was enhanced, in 1911, by the 13,000-ton sisters *Paul Lecat* and *Andre Lebon*. Trading via Suez out to Indochina and the Far East, their berthing reflected the diversity of the trade: 194 in first class, 145 second class, 109 third class and then, in a great jump, with 826 in steerage. Three additional versions, the *Porthos*, *Sphinx* and *Athos*, soon followed. The Dutch strengthened their colonial run out to the East Indies with the arrival, in 1915, of the 11,700-ton *Jan Pieterszoon Coen* of the Amsterdam-based Nederland Line.

Pacific passenger services grew as well and included the addition of the 13,400-ton *Niagara*, built for the Union Steamship Co. of New Zealand's extended service between Vancouver, Auckland and Sydney. Canadian Pacific Steamships dominated the run across the Pacific, between Vancouver, Yokohama, Kobe, Hong Kong and Shanghai. Two splendid three-stackers, the *Empress of Russia* and *Empress of Asia*, were built in 1912–13 for this trade. Their three-class accommodations included so-called Asiatic steerage. Japan's NYK Line (Nippon Yusen Kaisha) built five steamers but not for transpacific service, but on the long-haul run between the Far East and Northern Europe.

Evocatively named, the British India Steam Navigation Co. Ltd traded not only to India and the Persian Gulf, but to largely colonial East Africa via Suez as well. Union-Castle Line, also British, all but dominated the Atlantic route to South Africa and was joined by the likes of the Belgians to and from the colonial Congo and the Germans with their Eastern and Western African territories.

Union-Castle added its largest and finest liners yet, the 13,300-ton sisters *Balmoral Castle* and *Edinburgh Castle*, in 1909–10. Three-class ships, their first-class elegance was well known and included having the *Balmoral Castle* being also dubbed a royal yacht, carrying members of the British royal family to the opening of the South African parliament. But far bigger ships were ahead, namely the four-funnel sisters *Arundel Castle* and *Windsor Castle*. They were in fact the only liners with as many funnels to be built for a service other than the North Atlantic. While the first of the pair was laid down in 1915, their creation was long delayed by the war and so the twin 18,900-tonners did not come into service until 1921–22.

Unlike today's bustling cruise business to the sun-drenched, shop-filled Caribbean, passenger shipping to the West Indies and even Central America was quite limited in the years before the First World War. Service to South America was busy and prosperous, however, and included noted firms such as Liverpool-based Pacific Steam Navigation Co. to the West Coast of South America and the Royal Mail Lines to the East Coast of that continent. The Germans and the French also invested rather heavily in Latin American services from Europe.

British-flag Royal Mail Lines had a booming business between London and Southampton out to Rio de Janeiro, Santos, Montevideo and Buenos Aires. There was the British business trade coupled with masses of third-class migration collected at Spanish and Portugese ports en route. Great loads of cargo included Argentine beef brought home to Britain. Royal Mail added no fewer than six brand new passenger ships, beginning with the 10,000-ton *Amazon*, commissioned in 1906, and then, in an evolutionary pattern, the slightly larger *Araguaya*, *Avon*, *Asturias*, *Arlanza*, *Andes*, *Alcantara* and finally, at just over 16,000 tons, the *Almanzora*. Built

at Belfast, ships such as the 589ft-long *Almanzora* carried up to 1,400 passengers: 400 in first class, 230 second class and 760 in lower-deck third class. Some of these ships were also quite durable. The *Andes*, launched in May 1913, sailed on for thirty-nine years, until scrapped in Scotland in 1952. Her varied career included being a very celebrated British cruise ship in the 1930s. But Royal Mail was further enthused with Latin American trading and then constructed five 11,500-ton sisters, but to South America from Liverpool rather than London and Southampton. Also with great third-class quarters, they were the so-called 'D Class' – the *Deseado*, *Demerara*, *Desna*, *Darro* and *Drina*. Attending to the West Coast of South America and soon to use the newly opened Panama Canal, Britain's Pacific Steam Navigation Co., the Pacific Line, hoped to add five fine sisters beginning in 1913. The first two, the 15,500-ton *Orduna* and *Orbita*, were actually commissioned. The last three, the *Orca*, *Oropesa* and *Oroya*, were delayed by the war, however, and completed later.

From Germany, the Hamburg-South America Line traded to Rio and Buenos Aires, and was capped, in 1911, by their largest liner to date, the 14,500-ton *Cap Finisterre*. But further expansion was ahead: the 18,800-ton *Cap Trafalgar* was added in 1914 and was to be followed by the 20,500-ton *Cap Polonio*, but which was delayed by the start of the First World War. Spain's Compania Trasatlantica Espanola also added its biggest ships yet, the 10,000-ton *Reina Victoria Eugenie* and the *Infanta Isabel de Borbon*, for mid-Atlantic operatons: between Spain, Cuba and Mexico, and with occasional stops at New York en route.

French trading connections to Latin America were dominated by Bordeaux-based Compagnie Sudatlantique, which added its three largest liners to its service to Rio, Santos, Montevideo and Buenos Aires. At over 14,000 tons each, the *Lutetia*,

Shaw Savill Line's *Ceramic* was the largest liner to date on the Australian passenger run. (Albert Wilhelmi Collection)

The 12,000-ton *Corinthic* was primarily a big freighter, but with small first as well as second-class accommodations and mostly third-class quarters for Australia-bound immigrants. Built in 1902, she was operated by Shaw Savill. (Richard Faber Collection)

Gallia and *Massilia* carried passengers in four classes. Dutch investment was also heightened with the arrival of the 560ft-long sisters *Gelria* and *Tubantia*. Owned by the Royal Holland Lloyd, they traded between Amsterdam and ports along the East Coast of South America.

Plans for some new ships were complicated, however. At over 20,000 tons, the *William O'Swald* and *Johann Heinrich Burchard*, would have been two of the biggest, fastest and certainly finest German liners on the South American run

sailing from north European ports. They were being built for the Hamburg America Line, but then the war started and, in 1916, they were sold off to the Dutch, to Royal Holland Lloyd, becoming the *Brabantia* and *Lombardia* respectively. While eventually used in Latin American service, they were quickly found to be unsuccessful and then sold, by 1922, to the United American Lines, becoming the *Resolute* and *Reliance* respectively. But in some coincidence, they would be, in fact, bought back by Hamburg America in 1926.

The 12,500grt *Tamaroa* plied the run between London and ports in New Zealand, routed via the Caribbean and Panama. She was a classic blend of cargo and passengers (130 in all). (Shaw Savill Line)

Aberdeen Line's *Euripides*, completed in 1914 and used in Australian passenger service, became the *Akaroa* for Shaw Savill Line in 1932. This 15,000grt ship sailed for forty years, being finally retired and scrapped in 1954. (Albert Wilhelmi Collection)

Some ships, such as the freighter *Vedic*, belonging to Shaw Savill, were restyled with all-third-class, immigrant accommodations. (Richard Faber Collection)

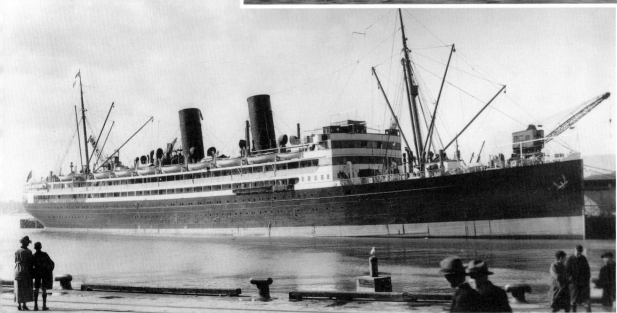

The 13,400grt *Niagara*, belonging to the Union Steamship Co. of New Zealand, offered an extensive transpacific service between Sydney, Auckland and then to Vancouver. (Luis Miguel Correia Collection)

Above Amsterdam-headquartered Nederland Line maintained a large fleet to and from the colonial East Indies, to the likes of Surabaya and Batavia. Here we see the 5,900grt *Grotius*, inbound at Tandjong Priok from distant Amsterdam. (Author's Collection)

Left Another Nederland Line passenger ship, but far larger, the 11,700grt *Jan Pieterszoon Coen* is also seen arriving with passengers, cargo, supplies and the all-important mail from Holland. This 503ft-long ship had quarters for some 390 passengers, divided in three classes. (Author's Collection)

Right Also in the Dutch colonial trades, Rotterdam Lloyd offered sailings from its homeport to Batavia and via Suez in ships such as the *Tjerimai*. (Author's Collection)

Below Liverpool-based Blue Funnel Line offered all-first class service out to Brisbane, Melbourne and Sydney aboard ships such as the 10,000-ton *Ascanius*. Catering also to the business and government trades, she carried up to 288 passengers, all of them in first class. (Alex Duncan)

From Marseilles, France's Messageries Maritimes maintained an extensive passenger fleet, trading to East Africa, south-east Asia and in the Pacific. The 510ft-long *Porthos* was used on the Marseilles–Saigon service, carrying freight, mail and up to 320 passengers. (Alex Duncan)

Regal in style, Canadian Pacific Atlantic liner services were complimented by transpacific service between Vancouver, Victoria and the Far East. That service was greatly enhanced and strengthened, in 1912–13 by the introduction of two fine three-stackers, the *Empress of Russia* and the *Empress of Asia* (shown here outbound from Vancouver). (Gillespie-Faber Collection)

The only four-stackers built for a service other than the North Atlantic were Union-Castle Line's 19,900grt *Arundel Castle* (shown here at Southampton) and her sister, the *Windsor Castle*. Ordered in 1915, they were delayed by the war and not introduced until 1921–22. They sailed regularly between Southampton, Las Palmas or Madeira and then down to Capetown, Port Elizabeth, East London and Durban. (Richard Faber Collection)

Portugal's *Nova Lisboa*, built in 1912, did double duty to colonial outposts. First, she was the *Albertville* for the Compagnie Maritime Belge and sailing between Antwerp and the Congo. Later, after joining Lisbon-based Companhia Nacional and becoming the *Nova Lisboa*, she traded between Lisbon and Mozambique as well as Angola. (Luis Miguel Correia Collection)

Clockwise from above
The big, 20,500-ton *Cap Polonio*, belonging to Hamburg-Sud, was one of the largest and most luxurious liners on the run from Northern Europe to ports along the East Coast of South America. (Author's Collection)

Royal Mail Lines' *Arlanza*, dating from 1912, is seen berthed at Santos. (Laire Jose Giraud Collection)

Another Royal Mail passenger ship, the *Andes*, is seen in this view dated 1919 at Buenos Aires. (Laire Jose Giraud Collection)

Some passenger ships, sturdy and sound, seemed to sail on forever. The 4,700grt *Ionia* began her days in 1913, just months after the *Titanic* sank, and then sailed on until 1965. She finished her days under the Greek flag, for the Hellenic Mediterranean Lines. (Alex Duncan)

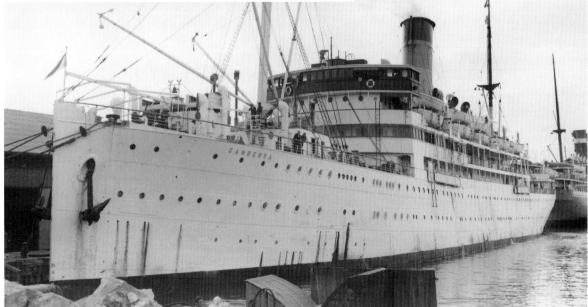

The little, 426ft-long *Canberra*, belonging to the Greek Line and used in the 1950s for transatlantic crossings, also began her sailing days in 1913. She had an extensive career and endured until scrapped in 1959. (Richard Faber Collection)

Even older, another Greek-owned passenger ship, the *Aegaeon*, was built in 1909 as Canadian Pacific's *Princess Alice*. She finally went to the shipbreakers in 1966. (Alex Duncan)

7

DISRUPTION & DESTRUCTION: THE FIRST WORLD WAR

They stood along the lower end of Hoboken's River Street, just north of the imposing Lackawanna Railway Terminal. For almost ninety years, they stretched for nearly three blocks. They were three stories high, but seemed taller and, in ways, with their red-brick façades, hinted of their original German ownership. Although largely rebuilt in the mid-1950s, there were touches to the very end of a sort of Teutonic gingerbread. But in the spring of 1996, in a merciless thrust of progress, urban renewal and rebuilding, several bulldozers reduced these one-time German ocean liner pierhead buildings to piles of rubble. The remains were quickly carted off. A direct link was gone.

Following the massive destruction in the Great Hoboken Pier Fire of 30 June 1900, these Hoboken piers were rebuilt, better and bigger and longer, by their joint owners, the Hamburg America Line and North German Lloyd. At the time, Hamburg America was said to be the biggest shipping company on earth. The four 950ft-long finger piers welcomed some of the largest, grandest ships then afloat – four-stackers such as the *Kaiser Wilhelm der Grosse* and *Kronprinzessin Cecilie*. In 1913, and bigger still, the *Imperator* – the world's largest ship by far – put into Hoboken. Great funnels and towering masts soared over the pier rooftops.

In the first dark days of the First World War, in the summer of 1914, and with America neutral until April 1917, a small fleet of German liners sat idle at these Hoboken piers. It was far too risky, according to strict military orders from Berlin, to return them to Hamburg and Bremen. In fact, they became extensions of Imperial Germany, moored representatives of the Kaiser, in the quiet, neutral waters of New York harbour. Pro-German parties and even fundraisers (to send monies, supplies & even medical needs to the Kaiser's armies) were held. The German crews were welcomed and looked after by local families. It was all quite ironic. But it was a rather hideous miscalculation that the mighty *Vaterland*, the Imperial flagship and

world's largest ship, was included in this otherwise idle Hoboken fleet. She seemed, in ways, to have been abandoned. In April 1917, as America entered the war, both the ships and the properties were seized by the US Government. The long-silent *Vaterland* soon became, as the greatest example, the USS *Leviathan*. She was now carrying Yankee soldiers who would fight and even kill the very Germans that had created her.

After the war, in the 1920s, cargo shipping very much dominated these Hoboken piers, but in the early '30s the Cunard Line suddenly needed an alternative terminal after one of their piers over in Manhattan's Chelsea section had burned down and had to be rebuilt. And so, for a time along lower River Street, legendary Atlantic superliners like the *Aquitania*, *Berengaria* (in fact, the former *Imperator*) and *Mauretania* called in at Hoboken. Some of the very last passenger ship visitors were the Greek flagship *Olympia* in the mid-'50s and the American liners *Independence* and *Constitution*.

These Hoboken piers were largely rebuilt (and with two new freight docks) in the '50s and then leased to the American Export Lines until 1970. The very last caller, an Indian freighter, cast off in 1979. Afterwards, there were fires, structural collapses and finally slow, staggered demolition that began in 1985 and then resumed three years later. The land area that once welcomed those floating palaces of yesteryear became, by 2005–06, a complex of offices, apartments, a high-rise luxury hotel, parkland and a marina. By 2010, when it was largely complete, it was a far different part of the Hudson River waterfront than that of 1910.

Like a great, dark curtain, the dramatic and very sudden start of the First World War in August 1914 threw commercial shipping, including passenger ships, into disruption, chaos and often subjected them to vast, senseless destruction. Those elegant grand saloons, gracious smoking rooms and inviting salons were now often

The classic-looking *Mauretania*, still the fastest liner afloat, is seen while in use as a hospital ship during First World War. (Albert Wilhelmi Collection)

Also in service as a large hospital ship, the *Aquitania* has been repainted in all-white and with the markings of the International Red Cross. (Albert Wilhelmi Collection)

crammed with bunks for troops or rows of metal hospital beds or stowed with boxed war materials. Almost all ships were called to some form of duty. Hundreds of thousands of soldier-passengers were moved across the seas – from the docks of Manhattan to the waterfronts of Brest and Liverpool, and on longer hauls, from Sydney and Capetown to Suez and even to and from tiny harbours in the eastern Mediterranean. It all seemed so different. The likes of wounded soldiers, lying in white-painted beds, were transported in the setting of the Adam Drawing Room aboard the all-white *Aquitania*, then being used as a huge hospital ship. Injured servicemen could gaze, in a sort of sentimental reversal, on the few remaining fittings from the vanished days of joyous peace. There was the carved marble of a fireplace and the copy of a Cipriani painting hanging above it.

The British lost a staggering 6 million tons of merchant ships in the first three years of war, up until 1917 (and then the war did not end for another year, until November 1918). Hard-hit, the Cunard Line alone lost thirty ships. The biggest vessels to leave the register were Cunard's great *Lusitania* and, a year and a half later, White Star's brand new *Britannic*.

The *Lusitania* remained, despite the worries of presence of sinister German U-boats, in a somewhat demoted commercial service. She ran monthly trips on the great Northern Route, on an extended, reduced-speed, eight-night schedule, between New York and Liverpool. On a sun-filled afternoon, 7 May 1915, however, she was torpedoed off the Irish coast by a lurking German U-boat. She sank in minutes, with a staggering 1,198 lives lost. The British were outraged, deeply shocked. Later, in deeper scholarship and more thorough research, a theory came to prominence that the British Government actually deliberately provoked the attack. With the loss of American lives as well, the purpose was simple and direct: bring the United States into the war against the Germans. In due course, it succeeded greatly. Millions of pro-German Americans no longer sided with the Kaiser and his forces. America entered the war two years later, in April 1917.

The sinking of the brand new *Britannic* was far more the loss of a large, important ship than a loss of life. Used as a hospital ship and wearing the colours of the International Red Cross, she was dispatched in the autumn of 1915 to the troubled waters of the eastern Mediterranean. She was the second largest Allied hospital ship with a staggering 3,300 beds in all. Her good works and courageous efforts lasted but a year, quite sadly, since she sank on the Aegean from a German-laid mine. In all, twenty-one perished. Back in London, realising the loss of the *Titanic* just four years before, White Star bitterly reflected that two of their three largest and finest liners were gone.

Heroic action! The *Olympic* was for a time, and like many other liners, 'dazzle painted'. In an extensive series of multicoloured geometric shapes, it was camouflage against prowling German warships, especially the ever-sinister U-boats. Barely in military service, in October 1914 the troopship *Olympic* attempted to tow the HMS *Audacious*, a mine-damaged battleship, while in the Irish Sea. But in the end, the warship was too badly injured. Finally, survivors were transferred over to the *Olympic*, towlines were cut and the military vessel allowed to sink. Later, on 12 May 1918, the liner was herself attacked by an enemy U-boat. Almost miraculously, the attack on the *Olympic* was foiled and then the liner managed to ram and sink the sub with the loss of all but one of her crew.

The French attempted to be cautious during the war. As hostilities began in the summer of 1914, the national flag, the four-funnel *France*, was hurriedly laid-up in the backwaters at Brest. Her value as an important Allied troopship was quickly realised, however. Transferred to the French Government and renamed *France IV*, she was soon sent off to trooping duties in the Dardanelles. In November 1915, at Toulon, she was converted to a hospital ship, complete with white hull and vivid Red Cross markings. Her lavish public rooms were converted to hospital wards and surgeries. She handled tens of thousands of wounded servicemen over the next two years before reverting to trooping duties in 1917. A year later, she ferried American doughboys back to New York and then, in 1919, began a post-war austerity service between Brest and New York.

After America entered the war in April 1917, German ships and properties in all US ports fell into their hands. These included a collection of liners at Hoboken, among them the giant *Vaterland*. Her German crew were quick to react and subjected the vessel to 'dockside sabotage'. Systematically, they removed essential parts of her engines, disconnected fuel and water lines and erased all signage of fixtures and directions. No detail was overlooked, it seemed. Live steam suddenly hissed from toilets and bilge water poured from shower nozzles. Even ropes and wires were deliberately knotted. The ship had to be redesigned with new blueprints and detailed information being purposely recreated. It was an exhaustive, time-consuming affair, but quite successful in the end. By July, the *Vaterland*, as the renamed USS *Leviathan*, was in service as the biggest troopship afloat, Allied

Renamed as the *France IV*, the French Line flagship is seen as a hospital ship used in the Mediterranean in a view dated 1916. (French Line)

or otherwise. But there was one last act of German sabotage. On her shakedown cruise down to tropical Cuba, it was found that the ventilating system was reversed and all but suffocated crewmembers in those warm weather waters. A young signalman found life at sea so unpleasant that he opted to become an actor instead. His name: Humphrey Bogart.

The USS *Leviathan* proved a heroic wartime addition, carrying some 110,000 soldiers to fight the last of the Kaiser's armies. Near-countless other German liners fell into Yankee hands as well. Of the early four-stackers, the big *Kronprinz Wilhelm* was now the USS *Von Steuben*. Her near-sister, the *Kaiser Wilhelm II*, became the USS *Agamemnon* while the former *Kronprinzessin Cecilie* was now the USS *Mount Vernon*. Hamburg America's 22,200-ton *Amerika* had only the slightest change, to USS *America*, while the larger 25,600-ton *George Washington* needed no change as the USS *George Washington*. Smaller, the 16,300-ton sisters *Cincinnati* and *Cleveland* were now the USS *Covington* and USS *Mobile* respectively. Another big German, the 24,500-ton *Kaiserin Auguste Victoria*, went to the British instead and later sailed as the *Empress of Scotland* for Canadian Pacific.

Some plans were greatly disrupted. Holland America, as an example, launched their biggest liner yet, the 32,300grt *Statendam*, at Belfast in the summer of 1914. But her construction was halted a month later as the war started. She was finally seized by the British Government and, in April 1917, completed, but as the troopship *Justicia*. Sadly, the 776ft-long ship had only a few short months. On 20 July, she was torpedoed and sunk off the Irish coast while on a voyage to New York.

Intended to be a passenger ship when she was launched at Belfast in 1914, this 697ft ship was, due to the needs of the First World War, finished instead as the *Belgic*, a large freighter for the White Star Line. She was converted, in 1922–23, to a liner, becoming the *Belgenland* for the Red Star Line. (Richard Faber Collection)

Casualty: hundreds of passenger ships were lost in that First World War – from torpedoes, fires, sabotage, even for target practice for the military. Hamburg America Line's 2,827-passenger *Cincinnati*, completed in 1909, was seized by the Americans in 1917 and became the USS *Covington*. Sadly, within a year or so, on 1 July 1918, she was torpedoed by a German U-boat in the North Atlantic and quickly sank. (Author's Collection)

The largest troopship of the war was the USS *Leviathan*, the 54,282-ton ship that had been Germany's *Vaterland*. She had been seized by the American Government while idle in New York harbour, in April 1917. (Author's Collection)

Another large German liner seized and then put to use by the Americans was the 25,500grt *George Washington*. Beginning in 1917, she was carrying lots of the infamous 'doughboys', but as the Navy-operated USS *George Washington*. (United States Lines)

8

AFTERMATH 1918–19: RESURRECTION & RECONSTRUCTION

Passionate devotion! The late Frank Braynard was the consummate ocean liner enthusiast. He wrote dozens of books about liners, sketched them, painted them, collected just about everything from them and even organised 'parades of liners' in New York harbour. He absolutely loved, it seemed, all passenger ships. To the very end of his days, he had unbridled enthusiasm, an almost boyish enthusiasm.

Frank's very favourite liner, however, was the *Leviathan*. She was a significant ship of the First World War and, afterwards, brought America itself into the superliner league. She had been, of course, a prize of that war, having been the German *Vaterland*, completed in 1914, but then seized at her New York harbour berth three years later as a prize of war. Down came the German colours and up went the red, white and blue. Mrs Woodrow Wilson, it was said, suggested the name *Leviathan*. She was the wife of the American President.

Wars, especially world wars, leave the world in disorder and chaos. It is much like disrupting a vast picture puzzle, the numerous pieces being tossed and scattered about. Indeed, the passenger ship business was out of order, much changed, as the First World War ended in November 1918. The cast, the great armada of passenger liners, had changed indeed. Some ships had new roles, were in other hands; others were gone, victims of war's senseless destruction. So, as 1918 drew to a close, the theme was direct: business had to be resumed and ships restored or replaced.

Germany was all but stripped of all shipping by 1918–19. Almost all the pre-war passenger ships were gone, sunk or given away to the Allies as part of the bitter pill of reparations. The huge *Imperator*, quietly idle at Hamburg throughout the war, was reactivated and did a short stint as the USS *Imperator* before being given to the British, to Cunard, to become the legendary *Berengaria*. The *Vaterland* was of course already in Yankee hands and was sailing as the USS *Leviathan*. The last

of them, the incomplete, 56,600grt *Bismarck*, was also allocated to the British, but to the White Star Line. With tears, regret and even anger, thousands lined the Hamburg waterfront on 28 March 1922 as the *Bismarck*, the intended pride of the victorious German Empire, sailed off to a new life. She entered commercial service in May 1922 as the *Majestic*, the largest liner afloat, but flying the Red Ensign. John Malcolm-Brinnin noted, 'The Allies had shuffled the German merchant marine into oblivion.'

North German Lloyd had been planning two important liners, the 34,000grt sisters *Columbus* and *Hindenburg*, just as the war started. Unfinished, they sat out almost a full decade before actually getting to sea. The 774ft-long *Columbus* was taken by the Allies as reparations and completed as the *Homeric* for White Star. Consequently, the intended *Hindenburg* was in fact rechristened *Columbus* and then, with Allied blessings, completed by 1923 for German-flag service to New York.

Another German liner, the four-funnel, 16,700-ton *Victoria Luise*, the former record-breaking Atlantic speed queen *Deutschland*, was a mechanically troubled ship. In 1919, the Allies did not want her. So, she too remained with the Germans, but as the much demoded immigrant ship *Hansa*. Even two of her funnels were removed.

There was a sense of moderation, even some caution, about trading conditions following the First World War. As the most prominent player, no British company planned to build new superliners, but instead more moderately sized ships were on the drawing boards. Harland & Wolff, the famed Belfast shipbuilders, produced a series of 16,000-tonners, for example, for general account. At least one went to the Dominion Line, another to White Star (two others went to Holland America). Cunard, along with the likes of the affiliate Anchor Line, looked to a long series of single-stackers that began with the 578ft-long *Cameronia*, which was launched in December 1919. Cunard's 19,700grt *Scythia* was laid down at the same time, then launched in March 1920 and finally commissioned twelve months later.

The Italians began creating a much stronger presence in the Mediterranean, with services to New York but also to South America. The 24,300grt sisters *Giulio Cesare* and *Duilio*, belonging to NGI, Navigazione Generale Italiana, were the largest Italian liners yet. The 635ft-long *Giulio Cesare* was laid down, in fact, in December 1913, but then delayed by the war and so not completed until 1922. The 1,500-passenger *Duilio* suffered similar extended delays. In another notation, Genoa-based Transatlantica Italiana had ambitious plans but that were disrupted by the war. They had planned Italy's first and only four-stackers, the 2,700-passenger *Andrea Doria* and *Camillo di Cavour*, for service to New York. They would have been Italy's largest liners yet, but together with the delays of the war and then the collapse of their owners, the entire project was shelved by 1919.

Americans, it appeared, wanted a stronger presence on the Atlantic and so formed the United States Lines. The bulk of their fleet would be ex-German passengers ships, all seized during the war. Meanwhile, on the long-distance and colonial runs, new passenger ships seemed to be at a temporary pause in the years just after the war. Fresh tonnage would begin to appear, however, in the 1920s.

The very end of the decade 1910–19 offered hope and possibility. The great Atlantic shipping lines were reviving and, as that mass immigration from Europe all but ground to a halt (caused mostly by US Government severe immigration quotas in 1924), tourism by Americans to Europe would soon boom in the years ahead. Indeed, something of the 'good times' would continue. The British, French, Dutch, Germans and Italians would create new, important ships, each of them increasingly large. It was not until 1929, more than a decade after the war's end, however, that the first new superliners would appear. Germany's 50,000grt *Bremen* and *Europa* began a new wave of competition, a fresh era for the 'floating palaces'. Another fascinating chapter in ocean liner history evolved. Without doubt, much more is to be written about the world's great passenger ships.

Right, from top
With the war over and the Germans in defeat, their ships were confiscated by the Allies as reparations. The mighty *Imperator*, used briefly as the USS *Imperator*, was awarded to Cunard and became the *Berengaria*. She is seen here at Southampton with an Imperial Airways flying boat in the foreground and the *Empress of Australia* in the distance. (Author's Collection)

The second big German, the 950ft-long *Vaterland* became the *Leviathan*, America's largest passenger liner and only superliner prior to the completion of the speedy *United States* in 1952. The *Leviathan* is seen here at the Ocean Dock at Southampton with the *Olympic* in the distance. (United States Lines)

Yankee luxury: a first-class suite aboard the restored and refitted *Leviathan*. (Cronican-Arroyo Collection)

Finally, the third big German, the incomplete *Bismarck*, was given over to the White Star Line and emerged in 1922 as their *Majestic*. The 956-footer is seen here in the King George V Graving Dock at Southampton, but near the end of her sailing days, in 1934. (Richard Faber Collection)

Opposite American tourism to Europe boomed in the 1920s. Due to immigration quotas instituted by the US Government in 1924, third class and steerage were replaced by more comfortable but affordable tourist class. Profitable days gradually returned. Here we see, in a moodful view, a departure for Cherbourg and Southampton from New York of Cunard's *Aquitania*. (Cunard Line)

An intended German liner (from 1914) that was sold to the Dutch began sailing in 1922 for the newly formed United American Lines (but under the Panamanian flag) as the *Resolute*. Atlantic liner services were steadily reviving and expanding. (Richard Faber Collection)

Norwegian America Line's 13,100grt *Stavangerfjord*, completed in 1918, was one of the first brand new liners to be completed following the end of the war. Seen here at a Brooklyn pier, this 553ft-long ship proved to be one of the Atlantic great veterans. She sailed until 1963. (Albert Wilhelmi Collection)

Slowly, German lines were allowed, under Allied restriction and other problems, to revive and restore services. One of the great four-stackers from 1900, Hamburg America's *Deutschland* was returned to service, but as the demoded, all-third-class *Hansa*. Now reduced with two funnels, she carried immigrants out of Germany. (Hapag-Lloyd)

The Germans slowly began to build new tonnage, which included some liners. The proposed *Hindenburg*, a 32,300-tonner begun in 1914, was completed after long delays in 1922 as the *Columbus*. She was the new flagship of the reawakening North German Lloyd. (Hapag-Lloyd)

In the 1920s, the future for all passenger shipping seemed bright and hopeful. New ships were planned with some being larger, faster and even more luxurious. Here we see the *Empress of Australia*, off and away on another Atlantic crossing. (Cronican-Arroyo Collection)

BIBLIOGRAPHY

Braynard, Frank O. & Miller, William H., *Fifty Famous Liners Vols 1–3*. Cambridge, England: Patrick Stephens Ltd, 1982–86.

Crowdy, Michael & O'Donoghue, Kevin (eds), *Marine News*. Kendal, Cumbria: World Ship Society, 1963–2010.

Devol, George & Cassidy, Thomas (eds), *Ocean & Cruise News*. Stamford, Connecticut: World Ocean & Cruise Liner Society, 1980–2010.

Mayes, William. *Cruise Ships* (revised edition). Windsor: Overview Press Ltd, 2009.

Miller, William H., *British Ocean Liners: A Twilight Era 1960-85*. New York: W.W. Norton & Co., 1986.

– *Great British Passenger Ships*. Stroud, Gloucestershire: The History Press, 2010.

– *Floating Palaces: The Great Atlantic Liners*. Stroud, Gloucestershire: Amberley Publishing, 2011.

– *Pictorial Encyclopedia of Ocean Liners 1864-1994*. Mineola, New York: Dover Publications Inc., 1995.

– *Picture History of British Ocean Liners*. Mineola, New York: Dover Publications Inc., 2001.

– *Picture History of the Cunard Line 1840-1990*. Mineola, New York: Dover Publications Inc., 1991.

Visit our website and discover thousands of other History Press books.
www.thehistorypress.co.uk